Pete Newell's
Playing Big

D1122180

Pete Newell
Swen Nater

Human Kinetics

Library of Congress Cataloging-in-Publication Data

Newell, Pete, 1915-
 Pete Newell's playing big / Pete Newell, Swen Nater.
   p. cm.
 Includes index.
 ISBN-13: 978-0-7360-6809-3 (soft cover)
 ISBN-10: 0-7360-6809-0 (soft cover)
 1. Basketball--Offense. I. Nater, Swen, 1950- II. Title.
 GV889.N495 2008
 796.323'2--dc22   2007019293

ISBN-10: 0-7360-6809-0
ISBN-13: 978-0-7360-6809-3

Developmental Editor: Leigh Keylock; **Assistant Editor:** Christine Horger; **Copyeditor:** Patrick Connolly; **Proofreader:** Jim Burns; **Indexer:** Betty Frizzéll; **Permission Manager:** Carly Breeding; **Graphic Designer:** Nancy Rasmus; **Graphic Artist:** Kim McFarland; **Cover Designer:** Keith Blomberg; **Photographer (cover):** Getty Images; **Photographer (interior):** Neil Bernstein, unless otherwise noted; **Photo Asset Manager:** Laura Fitch; **Visual Production Assistant:** Joyce Brumfield; **Photo Office Assistant:** Jason Allen; **Art Manager:** Kelly Hendren; **Associate Art Manager:** Alan L. Wilborn; **Illustrator:** Mic Greenberg; **Printer:** United Graphics

We thank Bellevue Community College in Bellevue, Washington, for assistance in providing the location for the photo shoot for this book.

Human Kinetics books are available at special discounts for bulk purchase. Special editions or book excerpts can also be created to specification. For details, contact the Special Sales Manager at Human Kinetics.

Printed in the United States of America   10   9   8   7   6   5   4   3   2   1

Human Kinetics
Web site: www.HumanKinetics.com

United States: Human Kinetics
P.O. Box 5076
Champaign, IL 61825-5076
800-747-4457
e-mail: humank@hkusa.com

Canada: Human Kinetics
475 Devonshire Road Unit 100
Windsor, ON N8Y 2L5
800-465-7301 (in Canada only)
e-mail: orders@hkcanada.com

Europe: Human Kinetics
107 Bradford Road
Stanningley
Leeds LS28 6AT, United Kingdom
+44 (0) 113 255 5665
e-mail: hk@hkeurope.com

Australia: Human Kinetics
57A Price Avenue
Lower Mitcham, South Australia 5062
08 8372 0999
e-mail: info@hkaustralia.com

New Zealand: Human Kinetics
Division of Sports Distributors NZ Ltd.
P.O. Box 300 226 Albany
North Shore City
Auckland
0064 9 448 1207
e-mail: info@humankinetics.co.nz

CONTENTS ━━━━━━

DVD MENU

Introduction

Moves

Getting Open at the Wing
Wing Moves
Getting Open in the Post
Low-Post Moves
Mid-Post Moves
High-Post Moves

Tactics

Two-on-Two Passing to the Post
Two-on-Two Ball Screen
Two-on-Two Down Screen
Three-on-Three

Scoring

Jump Shot
Hook Shot
Jump Hook Shot
Reverse Layup With Pump Fake
Behind-the-Basket Layup

Drills

Shooting Drills
Passing Drills
Movement Drills
Rebounding Drills
Defense Drills

Total running time: 68 minutes

PREFACE

Basketball, like every sport, has undergone many changes since its inception. Originally, a center jump took place after each made field goal, and extreme contact was allowed. The game became so physical that fencing was placed around the court to keep fans from getting injured. Hence, basketball players became known as "cagers." As the game continued to evolve, the center jump was eliminated, zone offense was introduced, and the game flowed more continuously from one end to the other.

Tall players who could move and score became prized assets. At a shade over 6 feet, 10 inches (208 centimeters), yet very coordinated and competitive, George Mikan of DePaul University was basketball's first dominant big man. Bob Kurland at Oklahoma A&M (now Oklahoma State), Mikan's slightly taller contemporary, was also very agile and active in leading his Aggies to NCAA championships in 1945 and 1946. The two centers not only prompted rule changes such as goaltending, but also convinced everyone that the big man was a key to winning.

Soon, every tall guy who could even lace a pair of sneakers became a "project" worth developing. The problem was that few coaches and even fewer players understood the techniques and tactics that were required to excel in the post.

Perhaps because I recognized at an early stage of my coaching career how significant effective post play was to a basketball team's success, I became a devoted student—and subsequently a mentor—on that aspect of the game. And I began writing things down long ago, anticipating that one day I would find the opportunity to compile my knowledge of post play into a book.

When I began writing, there was only one post position in the game—a true center. Premier pivot players such as Bill Russell, Kareem Abdul-Jabbar, Moses Malone, Hakeem Olajuwon, and Shaquille O'Neal have dominated games in their respective eras. But the many ways that the game has changed—at both ends of the floor—and the types of athletes playing the sport have greatly expanded the definition of *post play* and *post players*.

My Pete Newell Big Man Camp, started in 1976, and my Tall Women's Camp have changed through the years to reflect how widely applicable the skills of post play have become across player positions. Many present and future Hall of Famers have attended through the years, but now it's just as likely that a Tayshaun Prince, Shawn Marion, or Mike Dunleavy Jr. will sign up for a camp as it is that a Kwame Brown, Jermaine O'Neal, or Tyson Chandler will take part.

The camps' fame has spread throughout the world, and I have been asked to teach post play in many countries. But my days of traveling so extensively are over. Therefore, I decided it was time to create a book to share the many teaching points I've compiled and refined through the course of my career, along with a DVD to share the Pete Newell camp experience.

One of my early camp participants, Swen Nater, who is also a writer, offered his assistance on the project. After I was convinced that Swen and I were of the same mind concerning the principles of post play and teaching, and after Human Kinetics indicated interest in publishing the book and DVD we had in mind, the project was under way.

The result, *Playing Big*, goes beyond explaining *what* is important to teach and learn about post play; it also details *how* to teach and use the techniques and tactics that are essential to successful performance in the lane area. The book and DVD provide a complete prescription for players of various positions and sizes to develop into inside forces at both ends of the floor. *Playing Big* also provides instruction for coaches on how to work with their players to teach them the inside game.

As you'll see, at my camps, all attendees learn footwork and scoring from the wing, high post, and mid post. In fact, we teach offensive skills from the outside in. Even the seven-footers begin by learning moves from the wings, including moves that involve advanced ballhandling and footwork. Once the players' perimeter offensive skills begin to develop, we move the players into the post to work on almost identical footwork. We teach on both sides of the half court so that players develop ambidexterity of the feet and hands. Players who attend the camp become inside-outside offensive players. The DVD captures this camp experience for coaches and players who are not able to attend themselves.

Because of time constraints, the camps only serve to develop offensive skills. However, this book spans the whole spectrum of techniques and tactics used in post play. If it's relevant to "playing big," you'll find it here.

The game of basketball may change, but the team that does a better job of controlling the inside will always control the game. Players who learn how to use size, strength, and technical and tactical advantages against an opponent will always have the edge. It happens every day on every court where the game is being played.

KEY TO DIAGRAMS

① Guard

② Guard

③ Forward

④ Forward

⑤ Center

① Player with ball

Ⓒ Coach

X Opponent

⟶ Path of player

·······▸ Path of ball

⊢ Screen

CHAPTER 1

Post Play Today

Much has changed in the game of basketball since the days of Mikan, Kurland, and Russell. The term *center* has been abandoned or redefined to connote the tall or large player who is the leading inside scorer, post defender, and rebounder on the team. But the days of camping on the low block and guarding an opponent doing the same are long gone.

Changes in the center's role and even the label assigned to the role, however, have not diminished the value of players who fulfill those functions. A 2007 analysis of NBA player salaries revealed that those serving what most closely resembles the center role are the highest-paid players in the league. Kevin Garnett, Ben Wallace, Shaquille O'Neal, Yao Ming, Chris Webber, Carlos Boozer, Jermaine O'Neal, Zach Randolph, and Tim Duncan are among the most highly compensated.

But that list also includes Dirk Nowitzki, Elton Brand, Pau Gasol, and Shawn Marion. These are players who can rebound and guard a big man on the low post but can also step out on the perimeter for a three-pointer or drive to the hoop. And we've all seen the wide repertoire of post moves and defensive stops that smaller all-stars such as Kobe Bryant, Tracy McGrady, Dwyane Wade, Joe Johnson, and LeBron James use to help their teams.

Indeed, the ability to perform effectively in the post is even more essential in the modern game. Post play is no longer a duty that is relegated to a single low-post "center"; rather, any of the players that a team has on the court at one time may need to fulfill duties in the post. Let's take a quick look at how this came to be.

© Icon Sports Media

Shawn Marion is one of those players who performs well in the post as well as on the perimeter.

Changes in the Works

Through the 1960s and into the early 1970s, most offenses operated from a triangular formation in which the post player would receive an entry pass with his back to the basket and either distribute the ball to a teammate or make a move to score. To execute this type of offense effectively, a team needed a large and skilled player as well as a great deal of practice time to learn and develop the options that kept the attack flowing.

When Title IX became law in 1972, one of its unintended consequences was to reduce the amount of practice time available for boys at the high school level; limited facilities meant they now had to share court time equally with girls' programs. Shorter practice sessions meant less time for instruction and significant challenges in trying to master the triangle, single-post offense. With practice time greatly reduced, boys' basketball coaches saw a need to simplify the half-court offensive attack.

At about the same time, a coach named Bobby Knight left West Point to become the head coach of men's basketball at Indiana University. At West Point, Knight had used an offense called *reverse action*, which was more of a traditional system where the post player was allowed to make moves with the back to the basket. However, at that time, the rules for screening changed so that players were no longer required to allow three feet (.9 meter) of space for the defender to get around the screen. Knight took full advantage of this rule change and invented *motion offense*, a system where all players—including the center—screened on the perimeter to free cutters for open jump shots and backdoor layups.

Players in Motion

Motion offense took the country by storm. High school coaches immediately swarmed to Knight's coaching clinics to learn more about this revolutionary offense, which Knight was having great success with at Indiana. Coaches knew they had come upon something very difficult for a defense to guard and, more important, much easier for a coach to teach. This was an offense that worked well and could be implemented in just a few weeks. Coaches who did implement the motion offense experienced instant success; teams were not conditioned to defend against the amount of screening, cutting, and ball movement that took place in a single possession with the motion offense.

What these coaches didn't know was that they were changing the game of basketball—in essence, they were eliminating the role of the strictly back-to-the-basket post player through whom the offensive attack had previously functioned. In the motion offense, scoring opportunities were created mostly by effective screens, the proper use of those screens, and quick, sure-handed ball movement. As a result, players became more versatile and interchangeable (see figure 1.1, *a* through *d*). Fewer teams considered one-on-one moves by a designated post player to be a primary option. Every player—regardless of position—was asked to screen on the perimeter, cut, and pass. The traditional labels of center, power forward, small forward, shooting guard (or off-guard), and point guard applied only loosely, if at all.

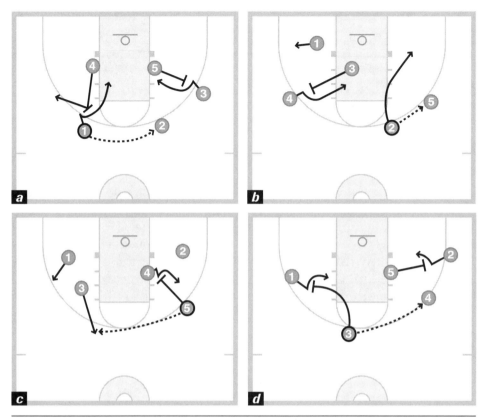

Figure 1.1 In this pure motion offense sequence, the middle is left open and scoring opportunities are created through screening, cutting, and passing.

Motion offenses moved the taller, bigger players farther away from the basket at more times during the game, both in executing the offense and guarding opponents' big players (who also set up in the lane area less often). That meant that those players needed to develop more mobility, better passing and receiving skills, and more accurate outside shots. The tall kid who could only operate inside was replaced by the smaller, more mobile, faster, and versatile player. These players were able to screen, cut, step out and pop the jumper, or drive to the hoop. They could also run the court and move quickly enough to defend a similarly versatile athlete on the other end.

Motion offense began to evolve quickly. The five-man motion offense—where all players (including the center) were involved on the perimeter—was altered by many coaches to adjust to their personnel. Some left two taller players closer to the basket while the three other players used screens to get free on the perimeter. This type of motion offense was called "two in and three out." This adjustment might seem like a step back toward traditional basketball and the use of the center

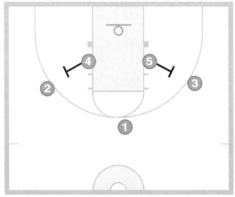

Figure 1.2 Two in and three out motion offense.

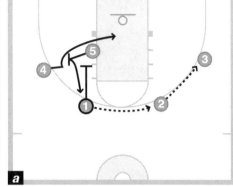

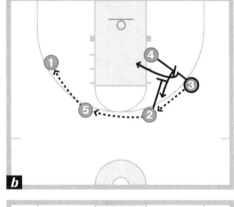

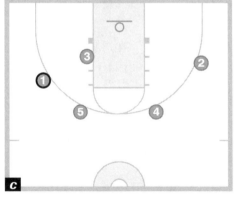

Figure 1.3 The basic movements of flex offense involve screening the screener on the weak side. One possible sequence is shown here.

close to the basket. On the contrary, centers were still screening on the perimeter (see figure 1.2); they just didn't stay there as long. The middle remained open for back cutting. If other teammates were cutting through the lane when a player received the ball inside, spacing became a problem and often eliminated the opportunity for any one-on-one moves except turnaround jump shots.

The emergence of the *flex offense* helped to complete the evolution of basketball from a game where the post player was the main character to a game in which player roles were less defined. More of a pattern-type offense than the motion offense, flex offense is a half-court offensive system where the baseline back screen brings a weak-side player into the open lane for the reception and score and brings all players even to the guard spots (see figure 1.3, *a* through *c*).

Though more structured, the flex offense does have at least one thing in common with motion offense—it takes the center away from the basket and, perhaps forever, changed the role of the post player.

More Players Into the Post

Coaches have always known the correlation of inside offensive play to success. As long as basketball is played on courts of the current size, with basically the same rules, the team that controls the paint will control the game. Although the three-point shot is popular, we have seen enough teams that rely on the outside shot to agree with the saying, "Live by the three and die by the three." Good coaches take advantage of the talents of their players. If a team has players who can operate inside, the coach should give those players opportunities to receive the ball close to the basket.

Some people may criticize the modern offenses for taking the traditional post out of the offensive game, and rightly so. But these offenses enabled coaches to take advantage of their players' talent by creating opportunities for more players to receive the ball inside and score. Forwards—and sometimes guards—who had inside skills were now eligible to move into the post, so that area was not unoccupied. When some players have size or strength advantages over those guarding them, those advantages should be exploited. That was true in the past and is also true today.

The challenge is that if more players on the team are going to post up, the coach must find the time and space to train those individuals on post play. On any given basketball team, male or female, the more players who become inside scorers, the more that team can dominate the paint—which is a key for team success.

Teaching post play for all positions is no longer an option—it's a necessity, not only for team success at the high school level but also for preparing players to play college basketball. As young people develop physically, the differences in size and strength become greater at the college level than they were in high school. Today's men's and women's basketball programs integrate post play for all positions into the half-court offense. High school coaches will serve their players well by helping them prepare to face the challenges of making a college roster. That means developing the post game of all players who show signs of the talent it takes to operate close to the basket. Coaches must find a way to do this, regardless of the limitations on practice time and space that many coaches face today. Creating a multidimensional team by developing multidimensional players has many rewards and should be the goal of every coach.

Planning for Sufficient Post Play

After assessing individual talent and evaluating the team roster, a coach can envision all combinations of players that might be on the floor at one time. Beginning with the combinations that offer the most team strength, the coach can then advance by creating additional groupings based on hypothetical situations. For example, by assuming that two specific players are in foul trouble, injured, or unable to play for other reasons, a new mixture is created.

Similarly, the coach can identify weaknesses in certain lineups. Perhaps a particular combination lacks rebounding prowess. And another might present too many defensive liabilities in the paint.

The next step is to develop practice drills to accentuate strengths and minimize weaknesses of any five-player grouping that might be on the court. For example, a challenging rebounding drill might pair up those players who have greater size, greater strength, and a nose for the ball. An inside scoring drill would match players of somewhat equal offensive and defensive skills.

On occasion, the coach might test a player in what appears to be a mismatch situation, just in case the team has to call on the player to help cover up a weak area. For instance, a smaller player might be more comfortable on the perimeter. But if the player has a longer reach, superior quickness, or excellent jumping ability, the player may be able to guard taller players. This player may benefit from practicing that role before being asked to step into it during a game.

When the coach develops practice plans designed to increase team depth through multidimensional player development, the team's sustained effectiveness in games will increase. In addition, as all players begin to improve their inside and outside play, the level of competition in practice increases. This can only serve the team well.

Conclusion

Playing basketball is fun. And the more things that players can do with the basketball—in more areas of the floor—the more fun the game is for them. That's why in off-season pickup games, centers like to go to the perimeter, and guards love to go inside and score. For big players, it's fun to be able to dribble the ball up the court and make one-on-one moves from the top of the key or the wing. For smaller players, it's fun to expand their game by posting up or by dunking the basketball. Today's players consider such versatile roles to be just a part of the game and an opportunity to use their full array of skills. The players and teams who best use their individual and collective abilities in all areas of the court—including the post—will be rewarded.

CHAPTER 2

Balance

Rarely does a player possess all the physical tools necessary for the ideal post game. Yet sometimes players or coaches will conclude that the absence of one or two desirable attributes renders an athlete incapable of excelling in and around the free throw lane. The faultiness of such a presumption is apparent by the outstanding success of many post players who are now in the Hall of Fame.

For example, Wes Unseld was a tremendous college center at the University of Louisville and then a five-time NBA all-star with the Baltimore/Washington Bullets. Wes stood only about 6 feet, 7 inches (almost 2 meters), was slow afoot, and was hardly what you would call a leaper. However, Wes compensated for those physical shortcomings by using his Mac-truck-like build, great understanding of the game, excellent footwork and positioning, and unrelenting determination to outplay more naturally gifted opponents. That's why coaches must not overlook those players who are less gifted physically when teaching the techniques of post play. And players who lack a certain physical tool needed to excel in the post must not get discouraged and fail to develop an inside game. Persistent players and patient coaches will eventually be rewarded if they continue to work at developing post skills, even when physical assets are less than impressive. From experience we know that if a player can catch the ball, has a desire to play the game, and is eager to learn and to work hard, the return is often worth the investment.

With that said, where do we start when it comes to developing the physical tools needed to succeed in the post? Chapters 2, 3, and 4 cover the first three steps—balance, footwork, and maneuvering speed. All three are skills that provide the foundation that players need for getting open, scoring, screening, rebounding, defense, and playing the game.

And within that foundation, balance is a prerequisite to footwork, and footwork to maneuvering speed.

Just as the atom is the basic building block of life, balance is the basic building block of basketball performance. Think about it. The efficacy of every movement a basketball player performs on the court is dependent on balance. Without good balance, no cut can be made quickly, no shot can be shot quickly, and no jump can be performed quickly. Above all, basketball is a game of quickness. If a player is off balance and needs to gain balance before moving, this results in hesitation. As we all know, "He who hesitates is lost." Nowhere is this principle more important than in basketball.

Because of the high degree of contact close to the basket, balance becomes even more important. Any player who enters the key area is subject to being pushed, pulled, and knocked around. In the key, players are generally more off balance than at any other area of the court. Therefore, proper balance is a must for any player playing inside.

Body Balance

Post players who have poor body balance, or improper weight distribution, will display some or all of the following symptoms: They stumble over themselves when stopping, starting, and changing directions; they are uncoordinated; they lack footwork and speed; and they are generally too upright. When you watch these players, you will notice that the position of the head is almost never between the feet.

Out of high school, George Mikan was not recruited by any college or university. When Ray Meyer began to work with him at DePaul, the first thing they worked on was Mikan's balance. Mikan was too erect. Without proper balance, the player has less control of the body. And if you don't have control of your own body, you can't handle your movement or the basketball. Body balance is fundamental to maneuvering and to mastering the offensive and defensive skills necessary for playing the game. As a general rule, taller players have a built-in disadvantage in this area when compared to players who are naturally lower to the ground; their center of gravity is higher, and they are not in the habit of bending the knees.

Proper body balance demands an equal distribution of weight on an imaginary line through the feet, hips, and head (see figure 2.1). The knees should be flexed to near 90 degrees, the back should be almost vertical, the head and chin should be up, and the feet should be spread a little wider than the shoulders. The arms should be positioned so that the upper arms are close to parallel to the floor and the forearms are vertical. This will help fend off the opponent. In other words, proper balance is attained when the player has established a low base with

Figure 2.1 Proper body balance.

the weight distributed evenly between the two feet; a little more than 50 percent of that weight is felt on the balls of the feet. If post players have their feet too close together, equal distribution of weight to both feet is nearly impossible. If the back is not close to vertical, too much weight will be felt either on the heels or, more commonly, on the balls of the feet. If the elbows are away from the body, balance will shift to one side or the other.

Proper body balance will allow post players to make quick movements and quick changes in direction. The flexed knees, proper positioning of the feet, low center of gravity, vertical spine, and elevated chin will ensure that the players can initiate movements quickly and make expected or unexpected directional changes. Proper arm position will help players accelerate quickly.

Regarding the development of body balance, the paradox is that the body must be thrown off balance in order to learn balance. When playing basketball, the post player is continually moving forward, sideways, backward, and upward—in other words, the post player is continually being thrown off balance. Therefore, when training a player for balance, we repeatedly throw the player off balance. The repeated cycle of losing and regaining proper balance is the only method of drilling in the habit of continual body adjustment.

However, before balance is tested, a player must first know what proper body balance looks like and, more important, what it feels like. Therefore, stationary balance is a prerequisite to moving balance.

Stationary Balance

When performing proper stationary balance, the knees are bent to near 90 degrees, the back is almost vertical, the feet are a little wider than shoulder-width apart, the elbows are close to the sides, and the hands are at about shoulder height. The head is directly above the midpoint between the two feet, and the chin is up.

Although the placement of the feet, elbows, and hands is crucial, the position of the head is the most important. For good balance, the head must remain above the midpoint between the two feet in order to maintain equal weight on both feet. The chin must be up to prevent too much weight from being shifted to the balls of the feet.

When the player begins to get the feel of proper balance, it's time for that player to practice initiating a balanced position. The player should practice moving into an upright stance and assuming a balanced position. At this point, the coach can look for errors in the player's positioning. Generally speaking, the most common errors are in the position of the head, the elevation of the chin, the width of the feet, and the verticality of the back. Most tall players have weak backs, usually demonstrated with a convex, or rounded, lower back.

The number of repetitions needed depends on the player. When a player can consistently achieve a properly balanced position, it's probably time to move on. However, this activity should be repeated daily until establishing balance becomes second nature.

Moving Balance

When a player shows signs that stationary balance is becoming second nature, the player may advance to developing balance in the context of moving without the basketball. Because jump stops and pivots have not been introduced at this point, the initial instruction of moving balance is limited to a simple operation called the Mikan drill, named after its founder, George Mikan. A description of the Mikan drill appears later in this chapter. Further information on training for moving balance is provided when footwork is covered in chapter 3.

Mikan and Duncan

George Mikan was the first truly great big man in basketball history. He was so dominant a player that when the Minneapolis Lakers traveled to New York, the marquee at Madison Square Garden read, "George Mikan vs. Knicks." On a side note, the story goes that when Mikan entered the locker room before that game, his teammates were still clothed in their suits and ties. They told him that since the sign said he was going to play the Knicks, he should go out there and do so. Although Mikan explained to his teammates that the publicity stunt was none of his doing and convinced them to suit up, he may have been capable of outscoring the Knicks by himself. While at DePaul University, Mikan did once outscore an opposing team in a game (his 53 points were more than the opponent, Rhode Island State, scored as a team).

Everyone knew that George Mikan "owned the paint." When we say "everyone," we mean his opponents and teammates. Mikan was so possessive of the area close to the basket that he once blocked a driving teammate's shot. As the story goes, a rookie drove the lane while Mikan was calling for the ball at the low post. Even though the player made a beautiful drive and scored, when running back on defense, Mikan told him to stay out of that area of the floor. When the obstinate player persisted, Mikan swatted his shot out of bounds. The rookie was traded the next day.

© Bettmann/CORBIS

In his era, George Mikan owned the paint.

Mikan is the main reason (along with Oklahoma A&M's Bob Kurland) that the goaltending rule was instituted. Before this rule was introduced, Mikan would zone the inside on defense and would jump above the rim to swat away shot attempts, whether the shots were on their way up or down. An aggressive player, Mikan tried to block every shot. And on offense, he constantly took the ball to the rim. When George began playing basketball for Ray Meyer at DePaul, he quickly became a star and was recognized as the best big man in the country.

When Mikan first arrived at DePaul, he reportedly struggled with balance because his posture was too upright. As with many tall youngsters, his lack of leg strength discouraged him from maintaining a lower center of gravity for very long. Ray Meyer put in many hours working with the young man who, fortunately, had a work ethic rarely seen in any sport. Needless to say, it was worth the time and effort. Ray Meyer helped Mikan develop into what the Associated Press described as "the greatest player in the first half century."

Believe it or not, Tim Duncan is not a gifted athlete. He is not an exceptional jumper and is not exceptionally quick. However, he is very effective at the low post because of his maneuverability, which can be attributed to impeccable balance. In the NBA, balance at the low post is very difficult to establish and maintain because of all the bumping, pulling, and pushing that go on near the basket. Duncan's lower-body strength and his ability to keep his center of gravity down allow him to keep his back vertical. This enables him to keep his head close to the position above the midpoint between the two feet. This posture is the key to Tim's ability to fake and step in either direction. Not only that, but because his back is vertical, he can use his length by elevating quickly. Being ambidextrous doesn't hurt either.

Drills for Balance

The following balance-training drills are simple. It will not take a player long to get the feel of proper balance. Though simple and quickly learned, these drills should be practiced daily for at least a few weeks. Coaches or players may be tempted to discontinue balance practice when improvement in play is seen. This must be avoided. Even the most experienced professional player (at any position) can benefit from regular balance training.

Push–Pull

While in a balanced and stationary position with knees flexed, players reach out to shake the hand of the coach. The coach proceeds to pull the players forward and push them backward, attempting to make the players move one or both feet (see figure 2.2). To maintain balance and not pick up the feet, players must continually use the coordination of the muscles. When a player moves a foot, the body learns and adjusts, which results in improved performance the next time.

Figure 2.2 A player being pushed and pulled to work on balance in the push–pull drill.

Hands Up

I believe our success at Cal was helped by the hands up drill. The concept of the drill was derived from the U.S. Marines, as each day the demand increased. We began with a duration of 2 minutes and increased it 2 minutes per day, until we had reached 20 minutes. I recommend a maximum of 10 minutes for high school players.

The squad disperses throughout the court surface, allowing plenty of room for moving around without bumping. Each player assumes a balanced and low position, with the knees well bent to place plenty of pressure on the thigh muscles. One foot is placed forward of the other, and one hand is up in the air, with the other arm parallel to the floor. Four commands determine the direction that the players will be sliding—right, left, forward, and backward. The commands are varied to prevent players from anticipating a pattern or tempo. All commands should be clear and loud. The coach also gives a command when he decides that the players should switch the position of the hands and feet.

I believe players must realize that extreme physical demands are important as games are won and lost at the end of the first and second halves of play. Although the drill is difficult and physically demanding, it has a tendency to cause team bonding. Players about to "hit the wall" must make a decision to quit or gut it out. Players in the best condition often cheer for and encourage those who are about to give up. Much to my surprise, for my teams, that support carried over to games, and the bonding holds to this day. I attribute that, in a large part, to the hands up drill.

The Mikan Drill

Although the components of the Mikan drill include more advanced skills than simple balance, we include it here because it is such a great drill for teaching balance.

The player begins by standing slightly to the right of the basket, 2 feet (about .6 meter) away from the backboard. The player's shoulders are squared to the backboard, and the player is holding the basketball, ready to begin.

The player shoots a right-handed baby hook shot off the glass, using the left foot to elevate (see figure 2.3). Immediately after shooting, the player grabs the ball out of the net and—without hesitation—shoots a left-handed hook shot, using the right foot to jump. Not allowing the ball to touch the floor and immediately shooting the second shot are key to developing balance. After shooting and landing, the player will be off balance. Players must get their feet back under them quickly in order to execute the second shot with fluency. During this drill, the coach should watch for errors; all of the basics of proper body balance must be regained after shooting—the feet must have proper spacing, the elbows must be in, the chin must be up, and the back must be in a vertical position.

Figure 2.3
Right-handed baby hook shot.

Conclusion

Basketball players should learn how to control their bodies before they try to learn how to handle the ball. Balance is the beginning of body control and is the first ingredient in building a solid base of operation. When players become sound in achieving proper balance, they can begin to master the other fundamentals of offensive and defensive play. Sound body balance is related to every aspect of offensive and defensive play and is the foundation on which all successful individual maneuvers are predicated.

Body balance includes footwork—the subject of chapter 3. Good footwork can only be achieved if body weight is properly and equally distributed to the feet. For that reason, balance development should be part of every practice session, from the first to the last practice session of the season. Emphasis should be placed on keeping a low center of gravity and maintaining the position of the head at all times.

Footwork

If a player plays the entire 40 minutes of a basketball game, that player will handle the basketball an average of about 10 percent of the game, or 4 minutes. However, the same player will use footwork for 40 minutes—while getting open, making cuts, handling the ball, blocking out, and defending. It is logical, then, to place a premium on footwork. In fact, without good footwork, a player will have difficulty making any maneuver, especially gaining possession of the basketball and making a move to get open and score once in possession.

Offensively, the post player's goal is to get an open shot. Although fakes and elevation are essential to good execution, proper footwork is required to move the body and create the space needed to shoot over a defender or to drive past that defender to the basket.

Defensively, moving the feet is essential to staying between the offensive player and the basket, moving around the offensive player to deny the pass, and getting into position to block the shot of a teammate's assignment who has managed to penetrate the defense. Defenders also need effective footwork when pivoting to block out an offensive rebounder and when moving to the rebound.

To master basic offensive footwork, players must learn jump stops, pivots, and spins.

Jump Stop

The ability to execute a jump stop while maintaining balance is an important feature of good footwork. For example, when catching the basketball, planting both feet simultaneously without moving either

Figure 3.1 Jump stop.

one gives the player a choice of pivot foot. The jump stop is executed when the player is moving or running toward the ball to receive it. The player takes off from the floor while in motion, jumps forward, and plants both feet on the floor simultaneously (as shown in figure 3.1). While executing this maneuver, the player must accelerate to the ball. That acceleration will test the player's balance when she comes to a stop, often causing a player to take a step—and thus lose one option as the pivot foot—to regain balance.

A proper two-footed jump stop is prerequisite to pivoting. As the player lands, the knees must bend to absorb the shock, resulting in a lower center of gravity. The impact of the landing is first felt by the heels and then transferred almost entirely to the balls of the feet. If the landing is on the balls of the feet, the gluteal and hamstring muscles—which are pivotal in gaining balance—are taken out of the equation. The player's back must be very straight. If the player is leaning forward, the body's momentum will continue forward.

Pivoting

Pivoting, or making a 180-degree turn while holding the basketball, is a maneuver that the post player makes often. Therefore, learning to pivot properly is important for several reasons. Proper pivoting prevents the traveling call, initiates an offensive move, protects the basketball from defenders who reach and attempt to steal it, and helps seal a defender away from the key area when being fronted.

Players should learn two types of pivots: the reverse pivot and the front pivot. Each type has its own purpose and function. When pivoting, a player's balance is tested. Therefore, the coach should watch for violations of proper balance, particularly the center of gravity, the distance between the two feet, and the position of the back, head, and chin.

Reverse Pivot

In low-post play, after receiving the basketball with the jump stop, the player executes the reverse pivot—sometimes called the *inside pivot*—by swinging one foot between himself and the defender and pivoting

180 degrees to face the basket (see figure 3.2, *a* and *b*). To maintain balance when turning, the player leans the shoulders slightly forward and keeps the center of gravity low. Many post players make the mistake of rising up when pivoting. This allows a defender to crowd in and force the offensive player back and out of balance. Making a quick offensive move at that point is nearly impossible. During the reverse pivot, the ball is tucked just below the chest and is protected by the slight lean forward. The player is ready to make the quick shot, drive, or pass.

Figure 3.2 Reverse pivot: The player *(a)* executes a backward swing of the nonpivot foot and *(b)* assumes the triple-threat position after making the turn.

Front Pivot

The front pivot is executed by swinging the nonpivot foot out and then toward the defender (see figure 3.3, *a* and *b*).

Because the reverse pivot closes the gap between the offensive player and the defender, it is more of an attacking move than the front pivot. That is not to say it is a better maneuver; the player should choose which pivot to use based on reading the defense. For example, when a player receives the basketball and sees that the defender is giving space, the

Figure 3.3   Front pivot: The player swings the nonpivot foot *(a)* out and then *(b)* toward the defender.

player can use the front pivot to shoot the quick jump shot. The front pivot gets the player in shooting position quicker. Players who are skilled at both driving and shooting from the low post often mix up the use of both types of pivots to keep the defense guessing. Furthermore, players should strive to become adept at using either foot as a pivot foot. This will allow them to pivot in either direction as they read the defense.

Spins

Spinning, or quickly rotating the body at least 180 degrees, causes a temporary loss of balance; the player must quickly regain balance to avoid falling to the floor. Offensively, spinning is most often used when the offensive player at the low post is being pushed from behind. In this situation, the defender is preventing the offensive player from stepping across the key or stepping to the baseline to make the move to score. The offensive player rolls—or spins—off the defender, toward the basket, and gains an almost immediate inside position. In essence, this maneuver is a front pivot, but instead of ending up in basically the same position, the player has moved toward the basket. As part of offensive counterstrategy, the entire move is covered in chapter 9; we will cover only the footwork here, without the basketball.

To help a player learn the spin, the coach (acting as the defender) gets directly behind the player and pushes on the player's back slightly

to one side. The player maintains a comfortable stance, shifts the weight more onto the heels, and straightens the back to an entirely upright position (see figure 3.4).

To maintain balance and not be pushed away from the basket, the player must use the defender's force. However, leaning back too much can result in a traveling call if the defender releases the pressure. Therefore, the player must first learn to maintain balance when pressure is released. With the player leaning back and the coach applying

Figure 3.4 Regaining balance after being pushed from behind.

force, the coach moves back and tests the player's balance. In this way, the player learns the maximum amount of counterforce he can apply without moving a foot on the release. When advancing to the teaching of the spin, the coach should periodically step back to make sure the player is still in a controlled and balanced position.

To execute the spin, the player rolls off the defender (to the side away from the maximum pressure) and literally falls in the direction opposite of the applied force. The player's shoulders and head are past the defender's waist, but the feet are still at the original location—although the spin has naturally caused the outside foot to pivot toward the spin (see figure 3.5). In fact, if the spin is done properly, pressure is released so quickly and entirely that the defender's force causes the defender to move away from the offensive player's direction; the two players are moving away from each other. Many young players make the mistake of spinning in a circle (like in a barrel), which limits movement toward the basket. The player must "fall" toward the basket, completely losing balance. To regain balance, the player must get the feet back under the head and come to a jump stop (see figure 3.6).

When working on this maneuver, much repetition is needed, and the player should practice spins equally in both directions. Daily practice is necessary until the coach is satisfied that repetition of the proper method has resulted in learning (the player can execute the move without conscious thought about its components).

One more detail can make a significant difference in the success of a player's spin. To gain a few more inches of penetration, the pivot should

Figure 3.5 Executing the spin.

Figure 3.6 Regaining balance after the spin.

be made on the heel of the foot rather than on the ball of the foot. Ten more inches (25 centimeters) can be the difference between an open shot and one that is pressured by either the defender who has caught up or a weak-side defender.

The Footwork of Kevin McHale and Dwyane Wade

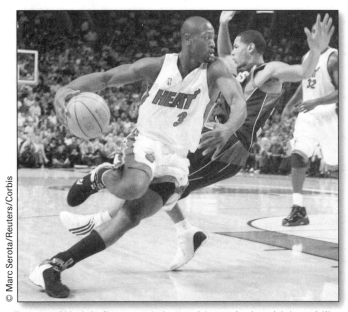

© Marc Serota/Reuters/Corbis

Dwyane Wade's first step is key to his explosive driving ability.

When today's players receive recognition for good footwork in the post, they are often compared to Kevin McHale, former Boston Celtic. Some people have even used the term *McHale-esque footwork* when referring to good footwork in the post area, especially pivoting and stepping through on an "up-and-under" move. McHale was best known for his up-and-under moves in the post—either faking a baseline jump shot (up) and then stepping across the key for a hook shot (under) or faking a jump shot in the key and stepping toward the baseline. It was not unusual to see Kevin use four or five fakes, both with the ball and with the feet, before making his move.

At the guard position today, no one has better footwork than Dwyane Wade. Although we would prefer his first step to be longer, that step is so quick that he seems to explode to the basket. His next two steps *are* big and enable him to elevate well. He often finishes a drive with a dunk.

But it is not the size of his steps, nor the elevation of his jump, that sets Wade apart when it comes to footwork while handling the basketball. His greatest strength while driving to the hoop is his ability to change direction and pace often, much like a running back. The best term we can think of to describe his driving is *explosive rhythm*.

Drills for Footwork

Do you remember learning multiplication tables by drilling? Not much fun, right? But quickly solving complex math problems *was* fun. We cannot forget that memorizing tables helped us solve the more complex problems.

There is no substitute for drilling and repetition when it comes to learning footwork. Significant improvement often means dozens of repetitions of the same maneuver. It takes faith on the part of the player. It takes a commitment to detail as well as patience on the part of the coach, not to mention constantly challenging the player to keep going and encouraging the player to believe that the work is worth it.

Jump Stop and Reverse Pivot

The player begins just below the baseline, where the free throw lane and baseline intersect. On the coach's command, the player sprints up the lane to the elbow of the key—that is, the intersection of the free throw line and the free throw lane (see figure 3.7). At the elbow of the key, the player makes a jump stop, maintaining proper balance. On the coach's next command, the player makes an inside (reverse) pivot so that the player is facing the baseline (see figure 3.8*a*). While making the pivot, the player should maintain a low center of gravity by keeping the knees bent, the back straight, the chin up, the hands a little higher than the waist, and the feet a little wider than shoulder width. On the coach's final command, the player runs toward the starting spot; just before arriving at the baseline, the player makes a change of pace and direction as if cutting by a defender (see figure 3.8*b*). This drill works best when more than one player is involved; immediately after the first player makes the cut, the coach signals for the next player to begin.

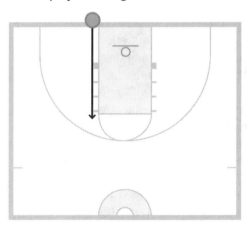

Figure 3.7 The player sprints up the lane and makes a jump stop at the elbow of the key.

Figure 3.8 *(a)* At the elbow, the player makes an inside pivot toward the baseline. *(b)* The player returns to the baseline and makes a cut, changing pace and direction.

Jump Stop and Front Pivot

In competition, the reverse pivot is generally used when a drive to the basket is the primary move. Conversely, the front pivot is used when the player sees that the immediate jump shot is available. Therefore, in the previous drill, when players make reverse pivots, they should maintain a crouched position with the ball tucked in so that they are ready for the drive to the basket. In this drill, the procedure is the same as in the previous drill, except that when making the front pivot, the player begins to bring the ball up for the jump shot. The front pivot is made by swinging the nonpivot foot away from the defender.

Spin to Jump Stop

The player may begin anywhere on the court. The player holds the basketball and assumes a low, balanced position, as if ready to make a low-post move. The coach plays behind the player and leans against the player's back, slightly to one side or the other. The player leans back to maintain balance and immediately spins, dribbling the basketball with the appropriate hand; the player then comes to a jump stop and, again, assumes a balanced position (see figure 3.9).

The coach immediately pushes against the player's back again, slightly to one side or the other. The player reacts and spins as before. The sequence is repeated so that the player will learn to read the defense quicker, improve the speed of the spin move, and learn to regain balance more quickly.

Figure 3.9 The player makes a spin move and regains balance.

Conclusion

Being in control when playing inside the paint is dependent on good footwork. By "good footwork," we mean footwork that enables the player to move effectively in either direction without conscious thought. Like balance, good footwork is developed through repeated practice, drilling both feet until the proper footwork is applied to all basketball maneuvers in the post.

Therefore, footwork must become a fundamental part of the practice plan. The coach should emphasize proper footwork and provide correction when necessary. This chapter only presents the basics of footwork. As we progress to getting open, using perimeter moves, and executing post moves, footwork is integrated into actual basketball maneuvers and therefore becomes more complicated. The basics described in this chapter are not sufficient for ensuring that advanced footwork will be executed properly. Season-long repetition and detailed feedback from the coach will help ensure that players develop this skill. The fruit of that labor will be realized toward the end of the season—and in the postseason—as players become less likely to commit traveling violations and more likely to execute quickly.

CHAPTER 4

Quick Maneuvers

We have all witnessed basketball players out of control in competition. For example, a tall player receives the ball 10 feet (3 meters) away from the rim and ends up traveling because he has never been in that situation. Or think of a breakaway layup situation. The ball handler has stolen the ball and is ahead of all the defenders on the way to the other end for an uncontested layup. From that point, it's just like the two-line layup drill that every team does when they take the floor for warm-ups. Easy, right? The player will move in a straight line to the basket, take the last dribble while simultaneously stepping with the foot that will be the takeoff foot, then take one and a half more steps and perform the layup. But there is something about having someone chase you that throws a monkey wrench into those simple practiced mechanics. During pregame layups, players run at slow to medium speed, and there is no defense. When chased by a defender, inexperienced players often move at speeds beyond their capabilities. What happens? The movements of dribbling hands and running feet become out of synch and uncoordinated, the ball begins to get away, and the player loses balance. This often results in the player losing the ball, stumbling, or attempting a very unorthodox layup. When a player moves so fast that control is lost, that player has exceeded his personal *maneuvering speed*.

Examples of players exceeding their maneuvering speeds are plentiful during freshman and JV basketball games, especially if one team is applying full-court pressure. In those games, the action sometimes consists of one player dribbling, another stealing the ball and racing toward the other end, only to have another player knock the ball loose from the blind side. This is followed by another player picking the ball up and racing the other way, and the cycle restarts.

The ability to maneuver under control at high speed is necessary for all players. In some basketball programs, it is imperative. Some coaches create up-tempo games because they feel that the higher pace is to their team's advantage. These coaches train their players to execute at high speed on offense; defensively, these teams try to force the other team to play faster than they are accustomed to. In general, taller players have more difficulty maneuvering under control at higher speeds; therefore, a taller player may see limited time when on a team that uses this up-tempo style of play.

Maneuvering speed can be defined as follows: "The fastest rate of speed that can be attained without losing the faculties of body control while accelerating, coming to a quick stop, and changing directions quickly." Any player who attempts to go beyond his personal maneuvering speed will lose control when attempting to do the three maneuvers mentioned. The player will stumble when accelerating, travel when coming to quick stops, and lose balance when changing directions too quickly.

As with reading, musical, or math abilities, all players have a personal potential for maneuvering speed. Generally speaking, the taller the player, the lower the maneuvering speed. The reason for this is primarily body balance. Taller players naturally have a higher center of gravity; therefore, jump stops, acceleration, and changes of direction are more difficult. For all three maneuvers, the lower to the ground the player is, the more successful that player will be. The potential maneuvering speed for tall players will never equal that of the guards and forwards. Fortunately, a lot can be done to maximize the maneuvering speed of any player. Many players, past and present, demonstrate the advantage of body control while at high speed.

Quickness is the most valuable attribute of the basketball player. Give me five players who are quicker than the opposing five, and I'll win—that is, providing that my five can execute at high speed. One of the quickest professional players today is Gilbert Arenas. In one-on-one situations, he can do things with the ball that most players cannot do without stumbling. His crossover dribble, fast drives, and quick pull-ups enable him, time and again, to get an uncontested shot up, even when defenders are bent on stopping his jump shot.

Gilbert's balance and footwork are the keys to his one-on-one success. His head is always up and positioned above his feet, enabling him to make quick advances, retreats, and changes of direction, all under complete control. Defenders who attempt to stay with him, step for step, soon lose balance. When Arenas senses that his defender is off balance, he pulls up for the jump shot. Rarely is his shot contested.

In the NBA today, no player provides a better example of speed under control than forward Shawn Marion. Baseline to baseline, Marion is as fast as they come. His high maneuvering speed and body control are

Through near-perfect footwork and balance, Gilbert Arenas maintains body control at all times.

displayed when he shoots layups. At the end of a fast break, Shawn can maintain full speed while shooting. Most players must decelerate when attempting layups on a fast break, but Marion is somehow able to keep his forward momentum from interfering with his touch. Again, he is able to pull this off through great footwork.

It is all about footwork. Chapter 2 presented balance as a prerequisite for being able to develop good footwork. And good footwork is the foundation on which maneuvering speed can be improved. Many great players were able to develop high levels of maneuvering speed because they had great footwork. How, then, does a player develop maneuvering speed?

Developing Maneuvering Speed

Coaches should be aware of each player's maneuvering speed potential and should track each player's progress toward improvement. The coach should also be aware of the impediments to a player's progress. This will enable the coach to generate personalized prescriptions. For example, some players have difficulty dribbling and running, while others may have difficulty cutting and catching the basketball without traveling. Drills must be created to help rectify issues that hinder individuals from making progress toward controlled maneuvering at game speed. Several good drills are presented later in this chapter. If necessary, coaches may modify and tailor these drills to their own players' needs.

However, although coaches should help players increase maneuvering speed in practice, they must not allow players to exceed their maneuvering speed in games. Practice is a time to push the limit, make mistakes, and improve, but the game is a time for playing under control at all times. Through practice, players will achieve increased maneuvering speed in games.

As mentioned, maneuvering speed must be developed in the following three areas: acceleration, quick stops, and changes of direction—in other words, starting, stopping under control, and changing directions. To provide a more clear idea of what these mean, we will explain all three maneuvers in the context of a drill. For lack of a better name, we will call this drill the "start, sudden stop, and change direction drill."

Players line up below the baseline, with the first player standing about where the baseline and the side of the free throw lane meet. On the whistle, the first player sprints and accelerates up the free throw lane and comes to a sudden two-footed jump stop at the elbow of the free throw lane. On the second whistle, the player makes a reverse pivot and faces the baseline. On the third whistle, the player accelerates toward the baseline, quickly changes direction, and comes to a sudden jump stop on the baseline.

Acceleration

Before the first whistle, the player assumes a position with a low center of gravity, ready to sprint. On the whistle, the player uses maximum acceleration and picks up as much speed as possible (similar to an Olympic speedskater or sprinter) before reaching just below the free throw line. Maximum acceleration is attained when the player's upper body gets too far ahead of the feet and the player begins to fall. The player does not initiate deceleration until just before reaching the free throw line.

Sudden Stop

The player must continue to accelerate as long as possible, making the sudden stop as difficult as possible. This cannot be overemphasized. In fact, the player should be going so fast that stopping under control at the free throw line may seem impossible. Nevertheless, when about to reach the elbow, the player comes to a two-footed jump stop. Balance is achieved by landing on the heels, staying low, and rocking into a balanced position. A low center of gravity allows for a more controlled stop and prevents falling forward after landing. If done properly, the player will have no difficulty stopping forward momentum after landing.

To allow the player to gain balance before pivoting, the player must hold position after the jump stop for about a second. Then, the player makes a reverse pivot while staying low.

Quick Change of Direction

The player begins the return to the baseline with a moderate amount of acceleration, but halfway there, the player changes direction by making a sharp 45-degree cut, either left or right. After the cut, the player accelerates as if attempting a quick move to the basket for a pass or making a crossover dribble drive. When arriving at the baseline, the player makes another sudden jump stop, testing his balance.

Drills for Quick Maneuvers

To increase maneuvering speed, a player must practice moving past present maneuvering speeds to the point where balance is tested. Moving to the next level can only be accomplished by experiencing it. Losing balance when stopping, pivoting, and changing directions should be welcomed during training. In time, players will become comfortable at the new speed. The following drills were designed to test maneuvering speed through combinations of starting, stopping, pivoting, spinning, and changing directions. Some are simple and some more complex. Increasing the complexity of a drill may also help players exceed their maneuvering speeds.

Start, Sudden Stop, and Change Direction With Dribbling

Players line up below the baseline. The first player in line has a basketball. On the whistle, the player accelerates while dribbling the basketball toward the elbow of the free throw lane. When approaching the elbow, the player comes to a sudden two-footed jump stop—maintaining balance—and tucks the basketball under the chin.

On the second whistle, the player makes a reverse pivot (the direction of the pivot is determined by the coach; the direction should be changed throughout the drill so that players develop ambidexterity). On the third whistle, the player passes the basketball to the next player in line (the type of pass is determined by the coach and, again, can be changed at any time). After passing the ball, the player immediately accelerates to the baseline, changes directions, and comes to a sudden jump stop on the baseline. While the first player is making the sprint and cut toward the baseline, the second player is dribbling and sprinting to the elbow.

Start and Stop

Players start below the baseline. On the whistle, player 1 sprints to the elbow and comes to a jump stop at the elbow. On the second whistle, player 1 sprints to half court and does the same, while player 2 is sprinting to the elbow that player 1 just occupied. The idea of the drill is for players to sprint and stop, sprint and stop, increasing controlled acceleration and body control when stopping.

Change of Direction and Stop

The player begins at one end line. On the whistle, the player starts down the court, making quick changes in direction every few steps. The player accelerates each time direction is changed. Periodically (four or five times while the player is cutting from one end line to the other), the coach yells, "stop." The player immediately comes to a jump stop. When the whistle blows again, the player resumes quick cuts and accelerations. The goal is to react quickly without losing balance.

Spin and Jump Stop

The player begins on one end line, facing away from the court. On the whistle, the player makes a spin move—spinning and falling toward the other end line—regains balance, and comes to a two-footed jump stop. On the next whistle, the player does the same. The player continues this pattern from one end line to the other. The objective is for the player to work on regaining balance after losing it. For the player to surpass his maneuvering speed, the coach must push him.

Conclusion

The more drills a player is involved in, the better the player's maneuvering speed will become, especially if those drills are executed at high speed. However, the best method for improving a tall player's maneuvering speed may be to include that player in group drills, especially drills that are sometimes reserved for guards and forwards only. For example, during games, tall players are typically not expected to dribble or defend one on one from the baseline to half court; these tasks are usually reserved for guards and forwards. However, a tall player can benefit from a practice drill that involves these tasks. The maneuvers required to handle the basketball and to defend advancement include the exact maneuvers that we've discussed in this chapter: acceleration, quick stops, and changes of direction. What makes this particular activity so valuable, especially defensive counteraction to offensive movement, is that it causes players to move beyond their maneuvering speed, resulting in lost balance and bad ballhandling. The players must then work on improving their control at those new speeds. A competitive spirit and continued practice will surely result in increased individual maneuvering speed.

Coaches should make each drill one of high intensity. When players are never allowed to "go through the motions"—but instead are encouraged to make every maneuver as if it were a game against last year's state champion—maneuvering speed will increase proportionally. In other words, coaches should take every opportunity to test maneuvering speed.

Maneuvering speed is the third part of the trinity of prerequisite skills for the post player. Improved balance allows for improvement in footwork, and improved footwork makes it possible for a player to improve maneuvering speed. It is now time to teach players how to use balance, footwork, and maneuvering speed to get open to receive the basketball.

CHAPTER 5

Moves to Get Open

With a good base of balance, footwork, and maneuvering speed, the player is ready to learn how to get open in the context of the offense. Offensive players know the positions they want. However, defenders are bent on preventing them from obtaining those spots. That creates a challenge for the offense and makes getting open an art. We call it an "art" because it requires creativity. Creativity for getting open to receive the basketball where you want it (whether at the wing or in the post) involves moving the defense out of position. Deceptive faking, quick cutting, and effective countermoves are the tools of creativity presented in this chapter.

I have found it more effective to teach post players perimeter footwork first and then apply virtually the same footwork to the post. Therefore, we begin with getting open at the wing. Please refer to the DVD when reading this chapter.

Getting Open at the Wing

To be able to execute the moves presented in chapters 7 and 9, a player must be able to get open at the perimeter against various types of one-on-one pressure defense. Because most offenses lack aggressive pressure release options, coaches have instituted defenses designed to play the passing lane, especially for entry passes such as the guard-to-wing pass.

Before the player makes a move to get open at the wing, the player should not be positioned on the block. The player should be positioned five or six feet (almost two meters) from the baseline and two or three feet (.6 to .9 meter) outside of the key (see figure 5.1). From this position, the backdoor threat is immediate, and the flash to the strong-side elbow is also available in case the guard is overplayed.

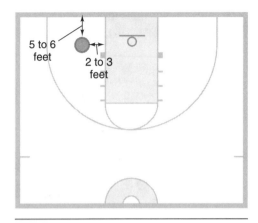

Figure 5.1 Proper positioning for getting open on the wing.

The goal of the offensive player is to receive the ball at the intersection of the free throw line extended and the three-point line. More detail on that subject will be provided in chapter 7 when we discuss wing moves.

We teach players four methods of getting open on the wing, all based on the following premise: The offensive player should never determine in advance how to get open; instead, the player must read the defense. All moves will be presented from the right side of the key but can be mirrored on the left side of the floor.

Move 1—Step Over Imagine drawing a line between the passer and the offensive post player. This line is referred to as the passing lane. The offensive player is positioned five or six feet (almost two meters) from the baseline and two or three feet (.6 to .9 meter) from the block, as mentioned above, ready to come out to the wing at the correct time. The defender is playing just below the passing line. After making a fake toward the basket to draw the defense in, the offensive player moves toward the ball by stepping over the defender's foot that is closest to the passer (see figure 5.2). The player now has a direct path to the three-point line with the defender blocked out. By stepping across the defender, the player is cutting between the defender and the desired area of reception—the wing.

Figure 5.2 Step over move.

Move 2—Circle   The defender, who is now concerned that the offensive player will step over the feet to create an easy catch at the wing, plays on the passing line or even slightly above it. To counter, the offensive player pivots on the right foot, brings the left foot behind the defender with a drop step (stepping toward the top of the key), and pivots on the left foot, bringing the right foot around to square up to the wing. The player then cuts out to receive the pass (see figure 5.3). Squaring up to the wing before moving there is crucial in making a direct cut from that position to the wing; because of the circular motion, players have a tendency to move toward the elbow before moving to the wing.

Figure 5.3   Circle move: *(a)* The defender plays above the passing line, so the offensive player *(b)* drop steps behind the defender, toward the ball, *(c)* squares toward the wing, and *(d)* cuts toward the wing.

Figure 5.4 The defender playing on the passing line.

Move 3—Pivot The defensive player has been burned with the step over and the circle methods of getting open; therefore, the defender is now establishing a position slightly below the passing line. The offensive player cannot step over nor circle. In addition, when the offensive player moves out to the perimeter, the defender continues to play on the passing lane, denying the pass (see figure 5.4).

In this situation, the offensive player makes a hard backdoor cut. If not open for the layup, the player puts on the brakes, pivots on the left foot (back pivot) to take a position between the defender and the wing (see figure 5.5), and makes a move to the perimeter to get open. Again, the player has established a position between the defender and the desired position at the wing.

Figure 5.5 Pivot move using a back pivot.

Move 4—Hands Up, Wing Some defenders are so concerned with playing the passing line that they purposely take their vision off the ball. When an offensive player senses this, the player can fake a reception to get open at the wing. To do this, the player raises the hands as if about to catch a lob pass (see figure 5.6). This fake can turn the defender's head, giving the offensive player enough time to cut to the wing and receive the ball. The fake reception must be convincing. The DVD contains great examples of just how to fake the reception.

Figure 5.6 The offensive player faking a reception.

Getting Open in the Post

The ideal positioning for low-post moves is at the mid post with the feet straddling the first line above the block. The offensive player's goal is to receive the ball there. However, the objective of the defensive player is just the opposite—preventing the post player from receiving the ball at the mid post. Therefore, the offensive player must use whatever means possible to take the defender out of position. Fakes, moves, and countermoves are used as the offensive player maneuvers to get to a position at the mid post—which we'll refer to as "position A." In the following sections, we present four situations where post players are attempting to establish position at the mid post: when cutting from the weak side, cutting from the top, using the flash cut, and maneuvering at the low post when the ball swings to the strong-side wing.

Getting Open When Coming Across the Key

Getting open coming across the key is more difficult than getting open in the post or when coming down the lane. When the offensive player is coming across the key, it is easier for the defender to stay in the passing lane. Setting the defender up through faking is crucial for success.

Move 1—Hands Up, Post   When positioned on the weak side and ready to come across the key, the player first reads how the defense is playing. If the defender is sagging to the ball, the offensive player makes eye contact with the ball handler, crouches down as if ready to jump, and then fakes the jump by rising up and raising one or both hands toward the basket area as a signal that the pass is open (see figure 5.7). The ball handler fakes an overhead pass. The reason for crouching is that it enables the player to maintain a low center of gravity. When the defender reacts to the lob threat by retreating, the offensive player must cut quickly to the open position at the mid post. Quickness is dependent on being low and ready.

Figure 5.7   The offensive player calling for the ball with one hand up.

This option must be a part of every low-post player's repertoire in order to achieve position at the mid post. In addition, weak-side defenders sag because they are concentrating on helping the strong side. A post player who is about to cut to the strong side can do a lot to reduce weak-side defensive help. The threat of the lob pass is an effective method of doing this.

Move 2—Fake and Cut   When the defender is sagging toward the ball and the offensive player makes a direct cut along the passing line, the defender will surely block that cut. To open a path for the cut, the player first makes a cut behind the defender, as if to go along the baseline,

Figure 5.8 The fake and cut move.

Figure 5.9 Clearing a path using the inside arm.

drawing the defender down. The player then changes direction and pace, cutting toward the ball (see figure 5.8). At the moment that the offensive player changes direction, the player slices the inside hand past the defender's head and toward position A. Do not underestimate the value of using the hand first.

After the player makes the initial cut, if the defender blocks the path to the ball, the offensive player continues toward the baseline, bringing the inside arm under the defender's arm to clear the path (see figure 5.9). The offensive player will probably not be able to assume a mid-post position, but since the defender is playing on the high side, the player may be able to receive a pass for a baseline power move (described in chapter 9).

Move 3—Fake, Cut, and Spin When an offensive player makes the fake and cut move just described (move 2) and the defender fronts with contact—preventing the offensive player from advancing—the player counters by spinning (see figure 5.10). Spinning involves swinging the baseline leg backward and then toward the passer. The player's back literally rolls on the defender's back.

When players receive the basketball in the low post, they should always make the catch while in the air and come to a two-footed jump stop with both feet landing simultaneously. This ensures that the player can use either foot as the pivot foot, which is crucial for leaving all footwork options open.

Figure 5.10   When the direct path across the key is blocked, the player drops the leg and spins around the defender.

When a player is making a move to get open, there is usually a point in time when contact begins. When coming across the key, contact is initiated when the offensive player makes the cut over the top after faking toward the baseline. Once contact has been made, the offensive player must do everything possible to maintain that contact so that the defender cannot make the countermove and get between the ball and the low-post area.

Getting Open When Cutting From the Top

This move is most often used when the half-court offense is in the process of being initiated. The basketball is already at a wing (or is about to be passed to a wing), and the post player is entering the key, attempting to obtain low-post position on the strong side.

This situation is challenging because the defender is waiting and there is no immediate scoring threat. However, that may be just what the defender thinks. What defenders may not know is that the threat of the lob pass is ever present. Seeing the defender waiting at the desired mid-post spot, the offensive player makes a hard cut toward the basket, calling for the lob pass (see figure 5.11*a*). If the defense reacts by retreating to the basket, the player makes a hard cut to the low-post area on the strong side by shooting the inside arm past the defender's shoulders and taking a long step (see figure 5.11*b*).

Figure 5.11 The offensive player *(a)* cuts down the lane and calls for the lob pass, then *(b)* makes a hard cut toward the strong-side low post and takes a long step.

Getting Open in the Key (the Flash Cut)

When the player is positioned on the weak-side block—with the ball at the opposite wing—the player anticipates a pass to the top of the key. The player makes a fake cut toward the baseline to deceive the defender into anticipating a cut all the way across the key (see figure 5.12*a*). This drops the defender down and opens up the middle. When the ball is passed and is almost to the top of the key, the player moves into the key by shooting the inside arm past the defender's shoulders (making slight contact if possible) and stepping across the defender's legs (making as much contact as is legally possible) (see figure 5.12*b*). The player's inside arm is already in receiving position, but the player will most likely contact the ball with the other arm first, because that arm is usually farther away from the defense (see figure 5.12*c*).

Figure 5.12 The offensive player *(a)* makes a baseline fake to draw the defender lower, *(b)* shoots the arm across the defender's shoulders and steps across the defender's legs, and *(c)* catches the ball in the key.

Getting Open When the Ball Is Coming to Your Side

When the ball is swinging to the side of the court that the player is already on, getting open should be less challenging because the defense is positioned behind the offensive player. However, some key tips can help ensure that the defense will be trapped behind the offensive post player.

The player should always face the opposite sideline until the ball is almost in the hands of the strong-side wing player (see figure 5.13). This will ensure that the defender stays on the inside. In other words, the defender will not attempt to go around (or front) the post player as long as that player is facing the opposite sideline. Offensive players at all levels often turn too early, allowing the defense to initiate denial defense. The turn must be made as late as possible.

When the ball is passed to the top of the key, the offensive player—having already made a small fake cut to the baseline—steps across the defender's legs and into the key, calling for the ball. Even if that player does not receive the ball, he is causing the defender to play to the high side, which is a very poor position when the ball is delivered to the strong-side wing. Note that the offensive player has still not turned toward the strong-side wing. The play is helped by a good pass fake from the ball handler.

Figure 5.13   The post player should face the opposite sideline until the ball is almost in the hands of the strong-side wing player.

When the ball is in the air between the top of the key and the strong-side wing, the offensive player performs the following three maneuvers to keep the defender behind: hit, step, and pivot. The moment the pass is made to the wing, the player places the baseline arm on the defender's shoulder closest to the half-court line (see figure 5.14*a*).

Almost simultaneously, the player steps with the baseline foot across the feet of the defender (see figure 5.14*b*). Now facing the top of the key, the player pivots toward the ball by lowering the center of gravity and sitting on the defender's thigh, freezing that player (see figure 5.14*c*). The rest of the play involves maintaining contact with the backside, keeping the upper arms parallel to the floor, and jumping to the ball to receive it.

Figure 5.14 Hit, step, and pivot: The offensive player *(a)* places the inside arm on the defender's shoulder and faces the opposite sideline, *(b)* steps across the defender's feet with the baseline foot, and *(c)* pivots and sits on the defender's thigh.

Receiving the Ball

When making the move to get open, whether it is across the key, down the lane, or when the ball is coming to the strong side, the "catch and score" play is ideal. If timing is perfect and the passer is ready when the move is made, the player, playing the post, may be able to catch the basketball and proceed directly into a move to the basket. However, the passer is not always ready, nor is he or she always confident enough to release the ball. Therefore, in many cases, the post player must hold low-post position and wait for the pass. To make things worse, the longer it takes for the passer to pass, the more advantage the defender has. In the catch and score, the defender is usually a step behind the offense. However, when the offensive player becomes stationary, the defender regains position, can better project when the pass will be made, and goes for the steal.

There are basically three ways the defender can play a stationary post: in front (between the ball and the offensive player), on the side, or behind. Therefore, the offensive post must learn three countertactics in order to be open to receive the pass: the seal, the rapid slide, and the foot war.

Sealing

Because of the amount of room to work with, a defender, if bent on getting between the ball and the offensive post player, will be able to do so. Some may view that as a bad thing. But if the offense is trained to pass the ball to the strong-side elbow in this situation, this defensive tactic may well work against the defender; when the pass is made from the wing to the high post, the offensive player can "seal" the defender away from the key and be wide open with a clear path to the basket.

For effective execution of the seal, just before the ball is passed to the high post, the offensive player quickly spins on the back of the fronting defender, maintaining contact and keeping the upper arms parallel to the floor and the hands toward the ceiling, called an "arm bar" (see figure 5.15).

Figure 5.15 The offensive player sealing the defender.

We call this the "arm bar" position. The proactive spin (turning before the ball is passed to the elbow), initiates contact and increases the chance of the post player sealing the defender. To help matters, keeping the arms in the arm bar position prevents the player from illegally arm-hooking the defender. When spinning, the player is concentrating on keeping the defender from going over the top.

To help ensure the safe reception of the ball, the offensive player must not leave too soon. Premature departure from the seal helps the defender get in between the ball and the player. If the player leaves when the basketball is almost directly in front of her, and then leaps to it, the defender is rendered hopeless. As a general rule, it is better to leave too late than too soon.

The importance of the seal in individual post work as well as in team play cannot be overemphasized. Defenders who get burned by the seal are more likely to concede good low-post position. In addition, when the seal is used, weak-side defensive players must often get involved, which opens up opportunities on the weak side if the ball is passed there. Sealing should be an integral part of an offensive post player's moves to get open and should also be an integral part of the team offense.

Quick Sliding

The second method of defending a stationary post is to play behind the offensive player, leave space, and, when the pass is made, make a quick move around to make the steal. This defensive strategy is used by quicker and lighter players who are at a disadvantage in a battle for position using the legs, body weight, and body strength. It can be very effective, not only because it can create a turnover but, equally as important, it discourages the ball handler from passing the ball into the post. For that reason, the offensive post player must transmit confidence to the ball handler through quick back-and-forth sliding.

When a player "slides," he or she lowers the center of gravity, keeps the back vertical, keeps the feet spread wide, and uses quick steps to alternate moving right and left. This helps prevent the defender from timing the steal. For example, the defender may see an opening around the left side of the player. But, through moving in that direction, the offensive player has changed the opening to the other side. This helps instill confidence in the passer that the post player will keep the defender behind and move to the ball when the pass is released.

The Foot War

As a general rule, the defensive post player avoids lower-body contact while the offensive player wants that contact. The defender avoids lower-

Figure 5.16   The defender (left) begins the foot war by stepping over the offensive player's foot and denying the pass.

body contact for two reasons: to keep the legs free to get into the passing lane, discouraging a direct pass into the post; and, if the ball does go in, to keep the legs free to stay between the ball and the basket. When both players work to achieve their goals, a "foot war" results.

With the basketball coming to the strong side, the offensive post player hits, finds, and pivots, making contact with the opponent's legs. Not acquiescing to this move, the defender releases leg contact and steps over the offensive player's leg in a three-quarter-denial position (see figure 5.16). The foot war has begun.

In order to regain lower-body contact to freeze the defender's legs and regain position between ball and basket (getting the defender behind), the offensive player uses the right leg to step across the defender's right leg. When doing so, the player locks the leg. Simultaneously, the player uses the outer thigh to make contact with the defender's inner thigh and apply horizontal pressure (see figure 5.17). This is different, and much better, than simply sitting on the thigh and applying vertical pressure, because in that situation, the defender may still be able to release. When done properly, the defender will not be able to lift the leg to free it.

When the foot war moves toward the baseline—when the defender is attempting to get into the passing lane from the bottom—the offensive post should maintain contact and keep the shoulders square to the passer. However, when the foot war moves up the lane, there is a point where the offensive player should release, spin, and cut for the basket, hoping to receive a lob pass (see figure 5.18). If that player does not receive the lob pass, a cut directly back toward the ball should make him wide open to receive a pass.

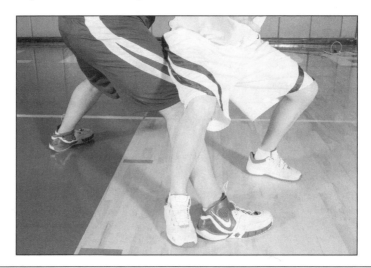

Figure 5.17 The offensive player places the foot across and over the defender's foot and places the hip on the inside of the defender's thigh.

Figure 5.18 The player releases when the lob pass is available.

Hakeem the Dream and Kobe Bryant

Who can forget Hakeem Olajuwon's agility that earned him distinction as the only post player in history to be listed in the "steals" category? Who can forget his oscillating and spinning footwork as defenders—time and again—were faked off balance and out of position, leaving Hakeem with a wide-open jump shot, hook shot, or layup? Who can forget the way he toyed with even the best defensive centers (who were no match for him one on one)? It seemed that he never used the same series of moves and countermoves twice in the same game. Hakeem Olajuwon was a master artist at the low post. Though Olajuwon was also noted for his shot blocking and rebounding, the NBA had never seen an offensive talent like Hakeem, nor has it since. Hakeem attended my Big Man Camp twice.

Yes, Hakeem Olajuwon was an unstoppable scoring machine. However, the skilled footwork he used for getting open was equally important to his effectiveness. Double-teaming a low-post player was rare in those days because the defensive rules were designed to display the individual moves of great offensive players. Therefore, emphasis on preventing a great offensive player from receiving the ball in his highest-percentage positions was even more important than it is today. Against some offensive players, especially those who were not creative and agile, that was not too difficult a task. However, those guarding Olajuwon had a most daunting assignment.

First, he had seemingly unlimited moves and countermoves. When the time was right, Olajuwon made his cut to the spot he wanted. If the defender was wise enough to cut him off, Hakeem used a series of pivots and spins to get to the spot anyway.

Second, Hakeem's scoring area was not limited to the low post. At times, while cutting to the block, he popped out to the elbow or high post. His 15-foot (4.6-meter) jump shot was deadly, and if a player was foolish enough to attempt the block, Hakeem's footwork to the basket was so good that a score was almost certain.

Third, Olajuwon was ambidextrous. Most players, even the great ones, have a strong side of the key—the side they are most effective on. Hakeem was equally effective on both sides, not only with the hands but also with the feet, and his team used him on both sides. That made the offense two times as deadly.

Why has the world not seen another Hakeem Olajuwon since? One reason is that talent like that seldom comes along. The other reason may be that our young players are not drilled in the ambidextrous footwork required to build a foundation for creativity.

Without question, the best player at getting open today is Kobe Bryant. Frankly, the fact that he almost always gets open to receive the basketball is miraculous, considering that opposing defenders are trained to keep the ball out of his hands. Like the Pistons' Richard Hamilton, Bryant's secret is perpetual motion.

John McDonough/Icon SMI

Although here shown dominating on defense, Hakeem Olajuwon's offensive skills were equally as great.

Arguably the best-conditioned athlete in the league today, Bryant is constantly moving without the basketball. But his motion is not activity without achievement. Playing the "cat and mouse" game (with Kobe, the mouse, attempting to get away from the defender), Kobe has one eye on the defender and the other on the basketball while faking, slashing, and cutting to set up his man. Every movement has a purpose, and the entire series of movements constitutes a calculated method for Kobe to create distance between himself and the defender at the moment the ball is able to be passed.

Like all players who excel at getting free and open, Kobe effectively uses the immediate pass and score close to the basket. Bryant uses the backdoor cut as well as anyone, and it is definitely a key to his ability to get open at the perimeter. But Kobe Bryant's backdoor cut for a score is not conventional by any means. If defenders are not alert, he will receive the quick lob for the dunk. This threat draws defenders even more toward the basket and, consequently, makes it just a little easier for Kobe to get open on the perimeter.

Drills for Getting Open

At the Big Man Camp, we use a progressive system of teaching players to get open, presenting each move followed by the countermove. I believe that demonstration is a key ingredient to good teaching; players must see a model of what is expected so they can imitate that example. Therefore, at the camps, we begin training with demonstration. My camp coaches and demonstrators are volunteers who have been involved in teaching post play for years. These individuals understand the big picture, but more important, they understand the little things that make defenders react and create openings for countermoves. Because they know what I think is important, they demonstrate just that—including details such as pointing the toe in a specific direction, taking the long step, dribbling with the proper hand, planting the foot for the Kiki move (see chapter 7), and squaring up the shoulders when springing back. The demonstrators also focus on footwork with proper balance so that countermoves can be made quickly.

Next, with the players in groups (preferably no more than six players in a group), each player takes a turn imitating what was demonstrated. During this activity, my demonstrators play defense and execute different defensive maneuvers so that the players must read the defense and react. At this point, we correct everything, especially footwork. No dunking is allowed because it hinders the development of ambidexterity and touch. We spend more time on this phase than on any other; learning to read the defense in a controlled situation greatly helps players to react when they go live. Moving on from this step too soon can result in players becoming frustrated when they go live. At this stage, we present several moves and countermoves.

The players then practice making all the moves without defense. For example, after all four moves to get open on the wing have been demonstrated and practiced, the players take turns cutting out to the wing, using a different move each time. In this way, the players are using imagination, a concept that I feel is key to learning creativity and developing habit.

Finally, players go live—one on one—while a coach provides them with corrective instruction. For example, if a player did not fake before cutting, the instructor makes the player and another coach aware of the error. While the next two players are competing, the other coach takes the player aside and explains the error. We also make use of a completely separate basket where a "pull-out" coach can work with a player for a few minutes if the player needs extra repetitions and instruction. After a time, that player returns to the group.

The Big Man Camp is a five-day event, specializing only in teaching players how to use offensive footwork to get open and how to read the defense to score. That format may seem difficult for college and, especially, high school pre-season programs with limited practice time. However, we feel strongly that these basics should be well-practiced before integrating them into drills that simulate game conditions and situations. In addition, these basic skills must be practiced daily. The automaticity we develop in the Big Man Camp in five days may take the coach one season. But that is not a problem. What is important is that footwork is practiced daily, because practice habits become game habits.

For example, proper footwork for getting open can be a part of almost every shooting drill. It should also be emphasized in five-on-zero offensive pattern practice. When the entry pass in the half-court offense calls for a guard-to-forward pass, wing players can practice any or all of the ways to get open.

Outside of the Big Man Camp, the following drill can help develop good footwork around the key.

Around-the-Key Cutting, Receiving, and Pivoting

Beginning in the low-post area, the player assumes a balanced position, with the hands about shoulder-width apart. The player fakes a cut under the basket, changes direction, and accelerates to the opposite low post (see figure 5.19).

When arriving at the other side of the key (and still moving with good speed), the player makes a sudden jump stop while catching an imaginary pass from the forward position. The jump stop is immediately followed by a pivot to face the basket as if ready to attack. The body is balanced with the knees bent, the back straight, and the imaginary basketball tucked under the chin. The player is in position to make the second move.

Again faking a cut across the key, the player quickly changes direction and speed and sprints to the free throw line, coming to a

Figure 5.19 The player fakes a cut, changes direction, and accelerates to the opposite low post.

sudden jump stop and pretending to receive a pass from a guard. Again, the player pivots to face the basket, ready to attack. A front or back pivot is acceptable.

With a destination of the original low-post area, the player begins the next maneuver by cutting hard toward the weak side of the backboard, as if to receive a lob pass. The next move is a quick change of direction toward the low post, where the player comes to a quick jump stop, pretending to receive a pass from the forward position. The jump stop is again followed with a pivot to face the basket.

When this drill is first introduced, the player should move at a speed that allows the player to successfully perform all parts of the drill. However, as skill increases, maneuvering speed can be tested by picking up the speed.

Conclusion

The methods of getting open presented here are only an introduction to the possibilities. No coach dreamed these methods up; players invented them during practice and competition. Since the inception of these methods in the Big Man Camp curriculum, I'm certain more effective ways of getting open have been invented. For example, I saw one forward get open on the wing by walking his defender from the low post to the elbow and then making a direct cut to the wing. It was ingenious. Because of the backdoor threat, the defender had to stay on the inside of the offensive player. There was nothing he could do to deny the pass once the player cut to the wing. When players learn to use creativity on the court, they often invent new and improved ways of doing things. Who benefits? The team.

With a good foundation of footwork for getting open, the next step is to learn how to receive the basketball properly. Chapter 6 will present some unique ways to ensure proper reception.

Receiving the Ball

For players to get the chance to dribble, pass, or shoot the basketball, they must first learn to properly receive the basketball. Countless scoring opportunities are lost because of fumbles. Half-court offensive timing is dependent on the movement of the ball and therefore dependent on successfully receiving the ball. Any hesitation will hinder the effectiveness of any type of play. For example, the fast break will no longer be a "fast" break if the quick outlet pass is not received properly. For this reason, passing and receiving are the most important offensive fundamentals. Without quick ball movement, great shooters will not be able to shoot when they are open, and players with great individual moves will not be able to make that move when the opening is there. Likewise, any player who is in the post will not be able to make the move when the opportunity arises.

The following principles of good receiving will help players and coaches understand the keys to the development of consistent and safe reception of the basketball. In this chapter, we also present an almost foolproof method for safe receiving, the "block and tuck" method.

Principles of Good Receiving

Over the years, we have had the opportunity to work with several players, big and small, who had challenges with catching the ball consistently. We say "opportunity" because there is no greater joy than to watch one of these players improve to the point where he is no longer a liability when put into the game. Following are eight principles of receiving that we teach to players. These principles are all of equal importance.

Figure 6.1 An outstretched hand presents a confident target for the pass.

Figure 6.2 Meeting the pass.

• **Maintain a low base of operation.** Proper body position for receiving requires a low center of gravity where the weight is equally distributed between the two feet. The player must be able to react to the pass by quickly moving in any direction necessary.

• **Present a confident target.** On the side the defender is playing, the receiver's arm should be at a 90-degree angle with the upper arm parallel to the floor. The hand is open, and the palm is facing the passer. The hand away from the defense is stretched up and slightly toward the passer. The fingers are completely stretched, presenting a confident target that says, "I want the ball, I will catch it when you pass, and I will do something good with it" (see figure 6.1).

• **Catch the ball in the air.** The receiver should always be in motion when catching the basketball. A stationary receiver is usually upright with stiff knees. That player is surely a liability to the team. A perfect pass is rare; usually the receiver needs to move to receive the pass without traveling. Generally speaking, the receiver should "meet the pass" while the receiver is still in the air (see figure 6.2).

• **Accelerate to the ball.** Players defending against opponents who are about to receive the basketball are usually accelerating. The problem is that receivers often decelerate just before making contact with the ball. Receivers should develop the habit of accelerating all the way to the catch. Not only will this help ensure reception, but because the defender may be lunging for the steal, it can also create a momentary window for the immediate reverse drive to the basket.

- **Come to a jump stop.** Coming to a jump stop—with both feet landing simultaneously—is the key to balance after receiving the basketball. The two-footed jump stop enables the player to use either foot as the pivot foot and allows the immediate execution of an offensive drive, shot, or pass. If only one foot is eligible to be the pivot foot, half the options are no longer available.

- **Catch the ball with the fingertips.** The fingers are the instruments of catching; the palm or heel of the hand should not make contact with the ball. As the hand makes contact with the ball, the target hand, being up and away from the body, moves slightly toward the body, with the ball (see figure 6.3). We call this a "soft touch." However, the ball should not be drawn too close to the body and within the reach of the post defender. The ball must remain away from the defense but not excessively far away from the body.

Figure 6.3 The receiver draws the ball slightly toward herself.

- **Move the hand with the ball just before contact.** It may seem contradictory that we ask players to move to the ball yet move their hands with the ball (or back toward the player) before contact. However, good receivers do both. They move to the ball to be alone to receive it. And just before the catch, to avoid hard contact between the ball and hand, they move their hands slightly back, making a "soft catch." Players who do this are often said to have "soft hands."

- **Catch with the intent to score or pass.** As soon as the fingertips make contact with the basketball, the receiver's head should turn in the direction away from the baseline and toward the action. The player is then able to read the defender and look for the pass to an open teammate.

Block and Tuck Method of Receiving

When catching the ball with both hands, skilled and experienced players usually catch the ball with the hands in reverse symmetry. In other words, the thumbs are pointing at each other, the left hand is in an "L" shape, and the right hand is the mirrored image of the left. A hole is formed between the hands that the player can see through.

This method does not pose problems for experienced receivers but may for those who are young or have special needs in this area. For those players, we recommend a method of receiving that is proven to improve receiving ability quickly and, in most cases, permanently. We call this method the "block and tuck" method. Seasoned players unconsciously use block and tuck when unable to catch with two hands.

When the pass is high and to the player's right side, the player "blocks" the ball with the right hand only (with the palm blocking the path of the ball) and then "tucks" the ball with the right hand into the left hand (see figure 6.4). The player ends up holding the ball under the chin with both hands while assuming a crouched and balanced position. Similarly, when the ball is passed high and to the player's left side, the player blocks with the left hand and tucks to the right hand.

When the ball is passed low and to the player's right side, the player blocks the ball with the right hand and tucks it into the left (see figure

Figure 6.4 Receiving a high pass to the right: *(a)* block and *(b)* tuck.

6.5). On a low pass, the player must bring the ball up to a position under the chin (as opposed to bringing the ball down under the chin when the ball is passed high).

Because it is common for tall players to have difficulty catching the ball, a coach should make sure that these players "see the ball into the hands." Taking the eye off the ball before it arrives causes most catching errors.

Figure 6.5 Receiving a low pass to the right: *(a)* block and *(b)* tuck.

Drills for Receiving

Drills can be used to help players develop proper and consistent reception skills. Repetition is the key to learning. However, we recommend a systematic approach where more complexity and challenges are presented as the player makes progress. First, the player should practice blocking and tucking while simply standing up straight. This will enable the player to place complete concentration on the function of the hands. The player should then progress through these drills in the following order.

Elton Brand

Much of Elton Brand's skill at receiving the basketball in a scoring area can be attributed to his training at Duke University under the direction of coach Mike Krzyzewski. No college coach is better at teaching post players how to use their lower bodies to gain and hold position, as well as how to use pivoting to reposition.

On paper, Elton Brand has all the essentials for getting open: great hands, long arms, and a strong lower body. But Brand has much more than that, thanks to Krzyzewski. For example, at Duke, when Brand was fronted at the low post while the basketball was at the wing, he was taught to seal *before* the basketball was passed back to the high post. Brand learned to anticipate the pass to the high post and trap the defender away from the basket early. This requires thinking ahead, and if done effectively, the "early seal" is a nightmare for a post

NBAE/Getty Images

Shown here blocking out for the rebound, Elton Brand uses the same technique when getting open to receive the ball.

defender. Elton Brand uses that type of anticipatory thinking and maneuvering throughout an entire offensive possession.

For receiving the basketball, Brand has all the tools. Throughout the maneuvering process, he maintains great position for receiving the basketball—his back is always straight, his head is up and alert, and his knees are bent to play at a lower center of gravity. He presents an inviting target, fully extending his receiving arm and completely stretching the fingers. Lastly, he has incredibly soft hands.

Back-and-Forth Passing and Receiving

The simplest passing and receiving drill involves two players passing the ball, practicing the eight principles described earlier. The types of passes thrown can progress from the two-hand chest pass all the way to the baseball pass. For more complexity, passes can be slightly high, low, left, or right.

Back to the Passer

The passer and receiver stand about 10 to 15 feet (3 to 4.5 meters) apart. The receiver has the back to the passer, is in a balanced position, and has the hands about shoulder-width apart (figure 6.6a). When the passer yells, "Pass," the receiver turns 180 degrees and catches the ball using the block and tuck method (figure 6.6b). When the receiver turns, the ball is well on the way. Coaches can adjust the time of the launch based on the ability of the receiver.

The passer should direct the ball to various areas so the receiver has to learn to find the basketball quickly and get a hand there to block the pass.

Figure 6.6 Back to the passer drill: *(a)* starting position; *(b)* the receiver turning 180 degrees with the hands up ready to block and tuck.

Ball Off the Wall

The receiver stands about 8 feet (2.4 meters) from a wall; the player is in a balanced position with the hands a little wider than shoulder-width apart. The passer is behind the receiver and about 20 feet (6 meters) from the wall. The receiver and passer are both facing the wall so the receiver cannot see the passer. The passer throws the ball against the wall so that it will rebound somewhere within the receiver's reach (see figure 6.7). The receiver uses the block and tuck method to receive the ball.

Figure 6.7 Ball off the wall drill.

Soft Hands Receiving

This drill must be done in a very quiet setting. Two players face each other and stand about 15 feet (4.5 meters) apart with one player holding a basketball. The pass is made to the other player, who attempts to receive the basketball in such a way that the contact between the hands and the ball makes no sound. The ball is passed back and forth. To make it a game, players can count soft catches and designate a winning number.

Conclusion

Proper receiving skills are prerequisite to executing the offensive fundamentals that require ballhandling. Players who have difficulty receiving the basketball safely and consistently often cause offensive systems to break down. For example, fumbles distort the timing of half-court offensive plays and fast breaks. Players who cannot secure the reception of a pass consistently are liabilities to their teams. The condition of having bad hands is sometimes called "fumblitis." Many basketball players—and players of all sports for that matter—are afflicted with fumblitis. What is it and what can be done? We divide fumblitis patients into two categories—those with weak hands and those with improper arm position.

Players with weak hands have minimum feel for the ball. Experience tells us that the proper prescription for players with weak hands is a combination of strength exercises and lots of practice catching the ball. Resistance exercises such as fingertip push-ups and using the weight roll-up bar can help improve hand strength; however, the actual practice of receiving the ball—in a controlled setting as well as in competition—is what enables the player to apply the improved strength. Through resistance training and practice, it is possible to turn weak hands into "soft hands." However, players afflicted with weak hands usually cannot be helped much.

Players with adequate hand strength who fumble because of improper arm position can be helped immeasurably. For those players, fumbling is often caused by the arms being below the waist rather than up in a ready position, and the hands being pointed downward. The fumble results from what we call "resistance receiving." Because the receiver must move the hands up to the receiving position after the pass is already in the air, there is no time to move to the ball. Consequently, the ball moves to the hands rather than the hands moving to the ball, and all the player can do is "resist," or block, the ball. In contrast, when the hands are up and ready, the player can extend the arms and move the hands to meet, rather than block, the ball. We call players who do this "receivers." Teaching players to provide a proper target is the key to changing "resisters" into "receivers."

The material presented up to this point in the book and DVD is preparatory for the one-on-one play presented at the Big Man Camp. The foundation of balance, footwork, and maneuvering speed—along with the skills for getting open and receiving the basketball—provide the groundwork for being able to get into a position to score. This is where it gets exciting. Players will learn exactly how to read the defense and respond quickly with the proper moves and countermoves to create the space needed to score.

CHAPTER 7

Wing Moves

I have always believed that a player with great talent but poor footwork can still be a good player. However, a player with average talent but great footwork can be an outstanding basketball player at both ends of the floor.

Without question, of all the centers who have played the game of basketball, the one blessed with the greatest combination of talent and footwork was Kareem Abdul-Jabbar. It is no accident that he was able to get off the "sky hook" quickly and uncontested. His impeccable foot and body faking repeatedly caused defenders to become off balance. Not only that, but once into the motion of his shot, he was able to read the defense and counter with reverse pivots.

Although not blessed with the talent of Kareem Abdul-Jabbar, an example of a current NBA player who has very good footwork is Andrew Bynum. When he participated in the Big Man Camp, I recognized right away that all he needed was footwork, maneuvering speed, and ambi-dexterity to be a very good professional player. Andrew worked hard and showed significant improvement in all three areas during the one-week camp. Although he may not become an all-time great, I believe that he will become a very good player before his career is finished.

Good footwork can make a player seem quicker than he actually is. A prime example of this is forward Kiki Vandeweghe, whom we will discuss later. The most valuable asset a basketball player can possess is quickness. I have seen it time and again. Through good footwork, a player of average quickness can make a quick defender look silly with great fakes, a quick first step, and countermoves.

In this chapter, we cover one-on-one offensive play from the wing. Players will learn to make the correct pivots when receiving the basketball and make the right moves after the pivot, depending on what the defense is doing. In chapter 9, we take most of that maneuvering and apply it to post play. In essence, we take the same moves and countermoves and show players how to use them in a more confined area, closer to the hoop. The DVD provides demonstrations of the moves described here. Learning can be enhanced by using the book and DVD at the same time and going back and forth between them. The moves presented in the following sections are the exact moves taught at the Big Man Camps, in exactly the same sequence.

One-on-One From the Wing

We start with the most basic element of one-on-one play—receiving the basketball the proper way. As we do at the Big Man Camps, we explain the reasons (the "why") for doing things a certain way. We proceed with read-and-react pivoting and then individual moves and countermoves.

Point of Reception

For moves from the wing, the best spot for receiving the basketball is at the intersection of the three-point line and the imaginary extension of the free throw line. Why? There are four reasons.

Reason 1—Spacing Between the Ball and the Low-Post Player   The first reason for catching the basketball at the intersection of the three-point line and the free throw line extended is because that location provides perfect spacing between the ball and the low-post player. Generally, the desirable distance between any passer and receiver is about 12 to 15 feet (3.6 to 4.5 meters). Outlet passing after a rebound and crosscourt skip passing are exceptions, but both are risky compared to a 15-foot (4.5-meter) pass. This distance is close enough to deliver a pass that has a low risk of interception; at the same time, it is far enough away to give the low-post receiver enough time to react and prepare the hands to handle the ball.

Reason 2—Three-Point Threat   Reason number 2 is obvious; catching the basketball outside the three-point line makes the receiver a three-point threat. This forces the defender to play the shot, making the pass into the post possible (the defender doesn't drop back). It also enables the player at the wing to initiate one-on-one moves by threatening the three-point shot.

Reason 3—Crosscourt Angle   With the ball at the intersection of the three-point line and the free throw line extended, a pass to the other wing (on the other side of the half court) is of much higher percentage than if the passer were closer to the baseline. The closer the line of the pass is to the baseline, the more bodies that are in the way—and consequently, the more possibilities for the interception.

Reason 4—Shorter Pass Back to the Point   The most dangerous pass in basketball is a pass from wing to point because a steal almost always leads directly to an uncontested layup for the opponent. At times, the steal occurs because a cunning defender anticipated the pass. But the most common reason is that the pass was too long. With the ball at the correct floor position, the pass back to the point is no more than 15 feet (4.5 meters), which is perfect for delivering a quick pass with plenty of speed on it.

Pivoting on the Inside Foot

When receiving the basketball at the intersection previously described, the player should catch the ball using a jump stop and face the passer. The jump stop enables the ball handler to use either foot as a pivot foot. On the left side of the floor, as explained earlier, if the defender plays tight at the reception, the player spins and drops the left foot directly toward the basket, initiating a reverse drive for the layup.

Reason 1—Closer to the Basket   If the defender gives space, the player uses the left foot as a pivot foot, swings the right foot around (front pivot), and squares up to the basket. Unlike a reverse pivot on the right foot, a front pivot on the inside foot will leave the player closer to the basket. After completing the front pivot, the nonpivot foot should be a little closer to the basket than the pivot foot. This alignment allows for a quicker first step if the player chooses to drive.

Reason 2—Drive the Defense Back   If the defender is playing tight at reception, and the offensive player uses a reverse pivot on the left foot, the defender will quickly close in. However, a front pivot on the inside, or right, foot attacks the defender immediately; if the defender closes in, this pivot gives the offensive player an opportunity to drive quickly by the defender to the baseline side.

Reason 3—Pivot Away From Pressure   One of the phrases heard most during the Big Man Camp is, "Pivot away from pressure." We are always trying to create space between the offensive player and the defender. Pivoting is one way to create space.

When receiving the ball under tight pressure, the player—after coming to the jump stop and facing the passer—pivots on the right foot, spins away from the defender, drops the left foot toward the baseline using a long step, dribbles the ball with the hand farthest away from the defender simultaneous with the landing of the driving foot, and drives toward the hoop. Making a long first step cannot be overemphasized. Two characteristics that separate the "special" offensive players from the good ones are a long first step and ambidexterity. The long first step makes a player of average quickness seem much quicker. That quick first step (if it doesn't lead to a direct score) drives the defender back and provides opportunities for a pull-back move (described later)—in other words, it creates that all-important thing we call space.

Reason 4—Step Left and Pass Left or Step Right and Pass Right After receiving the ball at the right wing (on a pass from the point) and executing a front pivot on the right foot, if the player chooses to pass the ball back to the point, the player simply needs to step with the left foot and pass with the left hand. If a reverse pivot on the left foot had been used, the player could not step with the left foot to pass because a traveling violation would occur. Crossing over with the right foot to pass is ill-advised; not only is it awkward, but the defense will jump right in front of the ball, knowing that the offensive player will not likely be able to cross back over for a drive. Therefore, players should pivot on the inside foot so that they can step toward the passer with the outside foot and pass with the outside hand. From the right wing, that means step left and pass left. From the left wing, it means step with the right foot and pass with the right hand.

Reading the Defense for Perimeter Moves

Beginning at the low-post block on the right side of the floor, the player steps in front of the defender with the right foot, pushes off with that foot, and accelerates toward the intersection of the free throw line extended and the three-point circle, creating space. The player receives the basketball from the point. Because the defender has left space, the player uses a front pivot and faces the defender.

Basketball is a game of counters. A team's offensive and defensive reactions are counters to what the opponent has presented. If a team offense is not designed to use counterstrategy against defensive tactics, that offense will be stopped. On the contrary, the team that is trained to read and react quickly will be unstoppable.

Reading and reacting in the one-on-one situation is no different. Players must learn to recognize what the defense is taking away—and thereby read what the defense is giving away so that the offensive player can take quick advantage. The following moves are all based on read-and-react strategy.

Move 1—Front Pivot and Drive Baseline With the offensive player facing the basket, the defender moves in and leaves room on the baseline side for the drive. The player crosses over with the left foot, swings the

Figure 7.1 After making a front pivot, the offensive player takes a long step past the defender and toward the basket.

basketball to the right hip for protection, and takes a long step past the defender and toward the basket (see figure 7.1). In most cases, in order to take the straight path to the basket, slight contact between the players occurs. That is good. The offensive player should brush the opponent, though not too much. The offensive driver must be aggressive. Contact favors the offense.

Move 2—Front Pivot and Drive Over the Top This move is made in the same situation as the previous one, but the defender is shading toward the baseline side, leaving just enough room for the offensive player to drive toward the middle (see figure 7.2). Footwork is a little tricky here because when initiating the drive, some players are tempted to pick up the right foot, or pivot foot, and cross over with it, using it for the first step of the drive. This should be avoided because it welcomes a traveling violation. The first step of the drive

Figure 7.2 The offensive player has just enough room to drive to the middle.

should be made with the nonpivot foot—the left foot in this case—and the dribble should occur just before the right foot hits the floor.

The move should end with a layup on the opposite side of the basket (a left-handed layup, jumping with the right foot). In games, a player may seldom be able to drive that far without encountering defenders along the way, but for training, ending with a layup is good footwork practice.

Move 3—Drop Step for a Layup   If the defender is playing tight and high when the offensive player squares up to the basket, the player pivots on the right foot, turns toward the baseline, takes a long step with the left foot, and drives to the basket (see figure 7.3). To help expedite the execution of this move, the player must be sure to keep the back as vertical as possible when turning. This will aid in a quick pivot around a vertical axis. Another important tip is that when the player is pivoting, the pivot foot should be turned to face the corner of the court. This releases the hip so the left leg can be free to point in the direction of the basket.

Figure 7.3   Drop step for a layup.

Move 4—Drop Step, Pull Back, Shot   The player is overplayed on reception and makes the reverse step toward the basket. However, the defender reacts and moves over and back to block the path to the basket. The player reads the defense and reacts by pulling the left foot back and regaining the original position (see figure 7.4). If the first step with the left foot was a long step, the distance between the offensive and defensive players should be great enough to get off a quick three-point shot. Once again, the coach should make the point about the importance of the long first step.

Figure 7.4   The player reacts to the defense by pulling back to the original position.

Move 5—Drop Step, Pull Back, Rocker Step Drive The offensive player makes the drop step, and the defender reacts by moving to block the path to the basket. However, the defensive player is moving back and has not completely blocked the path. The offensive player must now make another maneuver to create space. By rocking back toward the original position—and not moving either foot (still in driving position with the left foot stepping toward the basket)—the player makes the defender lean toward the rock. The player then reacts by pushing off the right foot and driving toward the basket (see figure 7.5).

Figure 7.5 The offensive player rocks backward, pulling the defender in the direction of the rock, then drives toward the basket.

Move 6—Drop Step, Pull Back, Explosion Step The offensive player has attempted to make the reverse drive, dropping the left foot toward the basket. However, the player reads that the defender has reacted quickly and has dropped back to prevent the drive. The offensive player reacts by pulling back to create space for the jump shot. Again, the defender reacts quickly and is closing in on the player. The offensive player—with knees flexed, ready to shoot, pass, or drive—counters by faking a crossover drive to see if the defender will retreat once more. The defender doesn't retreat (see figure 7.6), and the player takes a second, longer step toward the basket and beats the defender on the drive. We call the second step (the first step of the drive) the "explosion step."

Figure 7.6 After faking the crossover drive, the offensive player prepares to take an explosion step.

Move 7—Kiki Baseline 1   As mentioned, without question, quickness is the most important attribute a basketball player can possess, even more important than height. Shooting, jumping, and timing can all be taught (to a degree), but physical quickness is difficult to improve.

How is it then that, through the years, there have been players who were great but not quick? Think of Larry Bird, Kevin McHale, Bob Petit, and Magic Johnson. None of these players have ever been considered quick, but all were able to maneuver over and around their opponents. How was that? Perhaps a close look at another player will provide the answer.

At six-foot-eight (just over 2 meters), Kiki Vandeweghe was tall but not tall enough to just shoot over an opponent of equal size—and he was not quick afoot by any means. Yet Kiki was an NBA all-star two consecutive years (the 1982-1983 and 1983-1984 seasons) and averaged 26.7 and 29.4 points per game, respectively, in those seasons. If those statistics are not staggering enough for a "slower-than-average" forward, his field goal percentages for the two years were .547 and .558, unusual for the amount of points he generated.

High field goal percentages always result from open shots. But without natural physical quickness, how was Kiki able to produce open shots? Certainly his team didn't set screens for him all game. Certainly he didn't get those points off the glass. Kiki was known for his footwork, which enabled him to excel in the one-on-one game. His ability to drain the outside shot helped move defenders toward him. And, as someone once said, his shot fake was so convincing that even he went for it. Once he had the defender's legs straightening to block his jump shot, Kiki's first step on the drive was so long that it was equal to one and one-half steps for most people. Kiki's next two or three steps were normal, but by then, he was already on his way to the basket.

That first step did wonders for Kiki. His ambidexterity enabled him to finish with either hand and with a variety of shots. However, there were times early in his career when a defender was quick enough to put pressure on his jump shot and move with him on the first step. He needed a way to create space for his jump shot. Since necessity is the mother of invention, Kiki invented what has become known as the "Kiki move." This move is also called a "step-back" move. After taking the first step toward the basket and noticing that the defender was sprinting to catch up, Kiki used the foot closest to mid court to push himself back and away from the defender. The first time he tried this maneuver, he found himself wide open for the jump shot.

The footwork needed to pull off this countermove can be explained with three words: *in*, *side*, and *back*. On the right side of the floor, when the player drives toward the basket on the baseline side, the player steps *in* with the left foot. With that step, the player stops forward momentum. The player then steps to the *side* (and back) with the right foot and squares the right hip and shoulders to the basket, creating instant distance from the defender. Finally, the player steps *back* with the left foot to complete the maneuver and balance the body for the jump shot (see figure 7.7).

The Kiki move can be executed after one, two, or three dribbles. Within one or two dribbles, the offensive player will know if the

Figure 7.7 Kiki baseline 1: The offensive player *(a)* pushes back with the left foot, *(b)* drops the right foot back and to the side, and *(c)* shoots the jump shot.

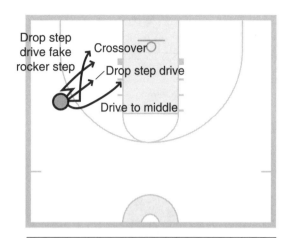

Figure 7.8 Kiki move driving lanes.

Figure 7.9 The offensive player uses the Kiki baseline 2 move to drive past the defender.

defender is cutting off the driving lane. The move can be initiated from any beginning stance. This includes the drop step drive, the fake drop step drive with a rocker step, the crossover move to the baseline, or the drive toward the middle (see figure 7.8).

Move 8—Kiki Baseline 2 Kiki baseline 2 is a countermove used when the defender reads the Kiki 1 and closes in on the offensive player. When the offensive player is stepping back during the Kiki 1 move and reads that the defender is moving in to stop the jump shot, the offensive player executes the Kiki 2 move. In this move, the player leans back on the right foot and then pushes forward with the same foot, accelerating past the defender and to the basket (see figure 7.9). Squaring the shoulders when stepping back is imperative for the quick countermove.

Move 9—Drop Step, Swing Through, Drive After receiving the ball at the intersection, the offensive player reads that the defender is playing tight and that the drop step drive is available as a countermove. However, when the player makes the drop step, the defender reacts well and moves over to cut off the drive. As a countermove, the offensive player steps back to create space, but not enough space is created for the jump shot. The move available is the "swing through and drive."

To keep the ball away from the defender's reach, the offensive player moves the ball from the right to the left side of the body (moving the arms like a pendulum, with the ball low to the ground). The player

Figure 7.10 Swing through and drive: *(a)* The offensive player drop steps to the baseline and is stopped by the defender; *(b)* the offensive player then swings the ball low from right to left.

takes a long step with the left, or nonpivot, foot and then continues in a straight path to the basket (see figure 7.10).

Move 10—Kiki Middle 1 Kiki middle 1 is a counter from the "swing through and drive" when the defender stops the drive by retreating and cutting off the driving lane. The Kiki middle 1 can also be an extension of any move that results in the player being positioned square to the basket.

Because the left foot is the nonpivot foot, it must be used for the first step in the drive to the middle, opposite from when driving to the baseline. The player begins with the left foot, dribbles, and then plants the right foot to stop momentum ("in"). The player retreats with the left foot ("side"), squaring the hips and shoulders to the basket, and moves the right foot back to square the feet for the jump shot ("back").

Move 11—Kiki Middle 2 Like the Kiki baseline 2, this is the counter-move to use if the defense reads the Kiki 1 step back. When the offensive player leans away from the basket—attempting to create space for the jump shot—if he reads that the defender has gotten wind of the move, the offensive player head fakes and rocker steps toward the basket for the drive.

Carmelo Anthony

NBAE/Getty Images

One-on-one, Carmelo Anthony is nearly impossible to stop.

The 2003 NBA draft was one to remember. The number one pick was LeBron James, number two was Serbian center Darko Milicic, and the third pick was Carmelo Anthony. All year, James was heralded as the heir to Michael Jordan, and that attention overshadowed what Anthony was doing in Denver. But not for those who knew the game. Under the radar, Carmelo turned the Denver Nuggets from the worst in the league into a playoff team. And although LeBron James beat Carmelo out for Rookie of the Year, Carmelo established himself as one of the most explosive scorers at the forward position in the NBA.

As a point guard, LeBron can dominate the basketball, while Carmelo has to work hard to get open. But once Carmelo has the ball on the wing, his offensive one-on-one skill surprises everyone. Carmelo is virtually unstoppable when guarded by one man. His three-point shot is so much of a threat that defenders have to honor it. This makes his shot fake extremely effective. And Carmelo takes full advantage when opponents leave their feet.

When driving to the basket, some players don't seem confident, and they finish by decelerating. This is not the case for Anthony. His first step is long and quick, but then he seems to continue to gain speed. He finishes with so much confidence, skill, and attitude that he ends up at the free throw line over nine times per game (where he shoots over 80 percent).

While Dwyane Wade simulates a halfback when penetrating the defense—jockeying, changing directions, and changing pace constantly—Carmelo Anthony is more like a fullback, seeing an opening and barreling through in an attempt to get as much yardage as possible. Anthony wants to get to the hole. But that is not to say that Carmelo does not have moves such as Kiki 1 and Kiki 2. On the contrary, what makes his drives all the way to the basket so effective is that he has the ability to pull back and shoot the short jump shot.

When it comes to offensive wing play, if there is a complete player in the NBA today, it's Carmelo Anthony. And he's only going to get better.

Conclusion

A coach was once asked, "What is the key to good coaching?" to which he replied, "Good players." Rarely, if ever, have we seen a team win a championship—at any level—with a roster where all players were average. It is certainly possible to have a very good basketball team without a "go to" player, but not a championship team. Basketball is a game of plays, especially on offense. Players make plays. All the coach can do is devise a system where players receive the ball in a position where they have an advantage that may enable them to score. But it is the player who ultimately has to make that play to score. That is the purpose of the Big Man Camp—to produce "scorers." There is no greater joy than to watch a player gain footwork skills, gain confidence, and become adept at reading the defense and scoring.

Teaching one-on-one basketball should not be limited to a one-week camp. Many coaches come to the camp to observe. When they get me alone, they often ask questions regarding little details of the moves. But some ask how they can integrate what we teach into their practices. That's when I become excited. If we can influence one coach to teach the footwork we believe in, we've influenced countless players who will be under that coach's supervision.

Although not a visitor of the camp, Tom Crean, current head coach at Marquette University, is one coach who believes that teaching "play making" is an irreplaceable part of practice. He has devised drills specifically to create gamelike situations that his players will face. These game situations are not limited to half-court offense. He even has players going one on one from half court, which simulates a fast break situation.

CHAPTER 8

Mid-Range and In-Lane Shots

Basketball is a game of scoring. Yes, defense is often the decider of championships, but ultimately, it is the team that outscores the opponent that wins. That means scoring is important. In today's game, more offensive players go into the mid-post area than ever before. We see guards, forwards, and centers take the inside position when a matchup or a defensive switch creates an offensive advantage in that area. Whereas tall players have usually gained skills for inside scoring by the time they become juniors in high school, the smaller players may not have. Therefore, coaches need to teach the inside offensive fundamentals, particularly the types of shots that work. Those shots include the running hook, the bank hook, the reverse layup, the jump hook, the jump shot, and layups when behind the basket. Players must be able to execute all these shots with both hands and from both sides of the basket. Learning the complete package, with both hands, equips the player to finish any move with a high-percentage shot.

Hook Shot

The hook shot has been around as long as the game. When shot properly, it's the most beautiful shot in basketball. We teach players three types of hook shots: the running hook, the bank hook, and the jump hook.

Running Hook Shot

A running hook shot is a shot where the shooter elevates from one foot and shoots with the opposite hand (for example, left foot and right hand). This shot begins with the player in a balanced position while holding the basketball just above chest level and away from the body (see figure 8.1*a*). The head is turned in the direction of the weak side in order to make the player a passing and scoring threat. To execute the hook shot, no dribble is needed. The move starts with a large step straight into the key. The step must be as long as is comfortable for the player. As the step is made, the player turns the foot so that when it is planted, it is parallel to the plane of the backboard (see figure 8.1*b*). The reason for this (the "why") is that this rotation unlocks the hip and allows the player to turn the shoulders. A locked hip will halt the turning of the body, making for an awkward hook shot, not to mention a shot going away from the glass. However, a move parallel to the plane of the backboard allows the offensive player to maintain, or initiate, contact with the defender, which is important for preventing the blocked shot. Post defenders need space to time the jump.

Figure 8.1 Preparing for the running hook shot: the player *(a)* at the low post in a balanced position and *(b)* stepping across the key with the stepping foot parallel to the backboard.

With both hands on the ball, the player lifts the ball to about the 2:00 position. The elbow of the shooting arm should be locked, with the arm completely straight. The off hand will naturally release, leaving the ball in the shooting hand (see figure 8.2a). From this point, the elbow never bends, not even at follow-through.

With the ball still behind the extended plane of the back, the arm moves toward the basket and follows to the floor (see figure 8.2b). The ball is released with a snap of the wrist, providing backspin for touch. The off arm should be bent to 90 degrees and should be parallel to the floor, creating space between the shooter and the defender. The shooter must not "palm" the ball; the ball should lie on the hand as it would for the jump shot. In this way, the ball will naturally leave the shooting hand just before the 12:00 position. As the player shoots, the shoulders should rotate and end up square to the basket. This will cause the feet to turn as well, landing square to the backboard and putting the player in good position to rebound if the shot is missed.

Figure 8.2 Running hook shot: *(a)* the ball in one hand with no bend in the elbow and *(b)* the arm following through toward the floor after the shot.

Bank Hook Shot

The execution of the bank hook shot is identical to the running hook shot with the exception that the target is not the rim but the corner of the rectangle located on the backboard. Again, the unlocking of the hip through the rotation of the jumping foot is important because it allows the rotation of the waist and finally the shoulder. Shoulder rotation permits the head to turn toward the target. The ball making contact with the corner of the square will determine the trajectory of the shot. If the ball is shot too high and soft, the ball may land on the six-inch piece of metal connecting the basket to the backboard. If it's shot too strong, the ball will overshoot the basket. The bank hook shot is used as a shot when moving toward the baseline and when receiving the basketball in the key while on the move.

Figure 8.3 The player is positioned for the jump hook shot.

Jump Hook Shot

The jump hook shot is used as a quick method of safely projecting the basketball toward the basket. Because this shot is executed while jumping off both feet, faking can be used effectively. Also, the trajectory of the shot can be adjusted to take advantage of a smaller defender or a shot blocker.

If the shooter is in front of the basket, the alignment of the feet is perpendicular to the backboard, and so are the shoulders. The player lifts the ball with both hands until it is well over the level of the head. When the nonshooting hand releases, it moves toward the basket and creates space for the shooter. The shooting hand lifts the basketball to about 1:00 (see figure 8.3). The body does not turn as it does for the running hook shot.

Reverse Layup With Pump Fake

As the result of a baseline move, a received pass, or an offensive rebound, the post player will often have the basketball close to the backboard on either side of the basket. The direct layup may not always be the highest-percentage shot; a reverse layup may often be the best option.

The player is facing the baseline, with the feet aligned parallel to the baseline, the basketball tucked under the chin, and the elbows out to create space. The body is in a low and balanced position. The player fakes the layup (pump fake), jumps toward the other side of the basket, and shoots a reverse layup with a degree of spin on the ball to take it back toward the basket (see figure 8.4). The basket is used for protection. Therefore, the player must be sure to release the basketball in the pocket—the corner where the backboard and basket meet. Even if either foot is eligible to be a pivot foot, neither should be moved before the jump because the official will surely make the traveling call.

Figure 8.4 After faking the layup, the player shoots a reverse layup.

Jump Shot

Positioned at the mid post at a 45-degree angle to the backboard, the player holds the ball under the chin with the shooting elbow touching the waist. The player is in a balanced position: the knees bent, the feet a little wider than the shoulders, the lower back arched in, the back in a vertical position, and the chin up. In other words, elevating for the jump shot requires no lowering of the body. Oscar Robertson is a prime example of someone with proper body position prior to the shot. His knees were always flexed, ready to spring up. His vertical back made it virtually impossible for defenders to gauge whether he was faking or shooting.

Figure 8.5 For a jump shot, the ball does not go behind the head.

Being ready to jump is important for the quick release. We teach players not to attempt to shoot over a defender; instead, they should shoot *by* the defender. The interval between the start of elevation and the release should be minimal. The jump shot motion begins when elevation begins, and the release is well before the peak of the jump. There is no time for taking the basketball behind the head; the ball must start toward the basket and maintain that course until the release (see figure 8.5).

Behind-the-Basket Layup

When making a move toward the basket, the post player will often end up in the area between the backboard and the baseline. In this case, a shot on the other side of the rim can be effective as the basket will screen the shooter from the defender. The behind-the-basket layup can be shot with a high percentage providing the player is able to use either hand. The choice of shooting hand is determined by which foot does the jumping. If the right foot is used, the left hand will shoot. If the wrong hand is used to shoot, the player will be out of balance, and the shot will be awkward.

Inside Shooting Hand

When shooting with the hand closest to the basket, the player jumps off the foot closest to the sideline (think of the elbow of the shooting hand lifting the knee of the same side of the body). The ball is elevated vertically into the nook between the basket and the backboard with no added spin. The natural position of the hand on the ball (slightly to the inside) will produce a natural spin that will take the ball off the backboard and over the rim (see figure 8.6).

Outside Shooting Hand

When jumping off the foot closest to the basket, the player raises and shoots the ball with the hand closest to the sideline. A little spin is required to direct the basketball over the rim after it rebounds off the backboard (see figure 8.7).

Figure 8.6 Reverse layup with the inside shooting hand.

Figure 8.7 Reverse layup with the outside shooting hand.

Touch

Shooting the basketball may be compared to driving, striking, or putting a golf ball. The golfer needs to master a variety of shots from different distances and angles. But all golfers know that beyond the fundamentals—and even beyond the amount of practice—the difference between the good and the great ones is "touch." By striking the golf ball in creative ways, the great ones can hook, slice, draw, fade, or even flop a shot. They can make the ball stop after landing, or even make it back up after landing. The great golfers can make the ball do what they want it to because of their touch.

Shooting a basketball is similar. The basketball player must master a variety of shots in order to take a high-percentage shot in every possible offensive situation. The coach may be able to provide direction when teaching the various shots, but it is up to the player to develop touch. Some people say touch is God given. You either have it or you don't. Like good hands, that may be true, but touch can be improved. It can be improved through experimentation and practice. When a player wants to become skilled at a left-handed reverse layup, the player practices that layup by experimenting with various degrees of spin and various angles. Players with great desire and passion will spend hours on one type of shot, hoping for one degree of improvement. That is how touch is developed.

Is touch God given? Is it true that you either have it or you don't? There are only three ways to find out—practice, practice, practice. After thousands of hours on the court, if touch arrives, you will know it.

Drills for Shooting

While attending DePaul University, George Mikan spent hundreds of hours practicing simple layup drills. At first, he probably saw daily improvement. But as he became more and more skilled, he had to work harder and longer for the same levels of improvement that he previously saw daily. The point is this: To become skilled around the basket, a player has to practice the following drills with faith that practice will pay off. These drills are not very exciting, but all are necessary to develop ambidexterity and familiarity with the basketball.

The Seven Shots

This drill has the player practicing all seven of the shots described in this chapter using right and left hands equally. The purpose of the drill is to develop ambidexterity, footwork, and skill in shooting the shots necessary for effective post play. This drill is timed by a coach, parent, or another player. The player must make 70 shots for the clock to stop—10 running hooks, 10 bank hooks, 10 jump hooks, 10 reverse layups with a pump fake, 10 turnaround jump shots, 10 behind-the-basket reverse layups using the inside hand, and 10 using the outside hand. It does not matter which hand makes most of the shots. The alternating of right- and left-hand shots is the important thing. The strong hand will teach the weaker how it's done. This drill is demonstrated on the DVD.

The player begins at the low post in position to begin shooting. On the signal, the player bounces the ball about two feet (.6 meter) away with reverse spin so it comes back. The player catches the ball and comes to a jump stop. Then, the player steps across the key and shoots a right-handed running hook. Make or miss, the player takes the ball, positions at the low post on the other side of the key, spins the ball back, and performs the same shot with the opposite hand. The player continues to alternate right- and left-hand shooting (shooting the running hook only) until 10 are made.

At that point, the player commences the next shot, which is the bank hook. Again, right- and left-hand shots are alternated until 10 are made. For this shot, the player does not reposition outside the key. Right- and left-hand bank shots are thrown up while the player stays close to the basket. This shooting is nothing more than the Mikan drill, explained in chapter 2.

Next, the player positions immediately to the left of the basket, but still inside the backboard, as if about to make a layup jumping off both feet. The player is facing the wall behind the basket. The player fakes a two-handed layup and jumps off both feet to make a reverse layup on the other side of the basket. (Neither foot can be lifted before the jump is made.) Right and left hands are used as the player alternates between the left and right sides of the basket until 10 shots are made.

Resuming low-post position and spinning the ball as before the running hook shot, the player makes a front pivot, faces the basket at a 45-degree angle, and shoots a bank jump shot. Shots are alternated from the left and right sides of the basket. Before each shot is attempted, the player must assume low-post position after spinning the ball and receiving it.

The next two shots are executed with the back facing the wall behind the basket. First, the player makes alternating left- and right-hand layups using the inside hand, or the hand closest to the basket. As the hand lifts the basketball toward the basket, the same-side knee lifts toward the ceiling as well. After making 10 layups with the inside hand, the player finishes the drill by making 10 with the outside hand, or the hand farthest away from the basket.

When all 70 shots are made, the clock is stopped, and the player is given the time it took to make them. Under three minutes is a very good time, and all players should strive to reach that mark at some point during the season.

Figure-Eight Hook Shot

We make no apology for promoting the running hook shot as the most dangerous weapon a post player can possess, even though some may label it "old school." The leading point producer of all time, Kareem Abdul-Jabbar, used it as his primary weapon, and we can safely say that he would be equally effective with it today. Any player will be a better player if the running hook shot is part of his arsenal. For this reason, a drill was created to help develop the running hook with both hands. The look of this drill is similar to the first shot in the seven shots drill, but with one difference—the player does not reposition at the low post in preparation for the next shot.

After shooting the first running hook shot across the key, the player takes the ball out of the basket, jogs to the opposite side of the key, steps outside the key, and immediately steps across the key to shoot the hook with the other hand. In other words, the player does not spin the ball and receive it with a jump stop before shooting. When performed correctly, this drill looks as if the player is continuously jogging while making left- and right-handed hook shots.

When using this drill in the off-season, a player should begin by shooting (not making) 100 hook shots for about a week or so and then progress to 200. There have been reports of some players shooting up to 500 hook shots per day for an entire off-season. During the season, this drill can be done before the start of a practice session.

Under-the-Basket Layup

This drill features two shots contained in the seven shots drill presented earlier in this section. The player will make 10 behind-the-basket reverse layups using the inside hand and 10 using the outside hand.

Conclusion

When recruiting players for college basketball, besides looking for a high level of quickness, I place a lot of importance on shooting. Generally, if a player can shoot the ball well, I can probably teach that player the rest. As a coach, it is easy to get wrapped up in having the players practice team plays and team defense. As a player, it is easy to get wrapped up in dunking the basketball and making fancy moves. All of those things are important (except the fancy moves), but we must not forget about developing touch. When coaching, I was convinced of the importance of focusing on shooting during practice. We probably spent as much time practicing game shots as any other part of the game.

This is in accordance with the whole-part method of teaching presented in chapter 15. We must teach the whole, teach the parts of that whole, and then put the "whole" thing back together. For example, when teaching full-court defense, the team is divided into the following three sections: the front line, the mid line, and the back line. The front line, usually two players, practices preventing the inbounds pass and penetration. The mid-line players practice discouraging the pass to the middle and stealing the ball when the opportunity comes. The back line works on stopping a two-on-one and stealing the long pass. After part work, the front and mid lines are combined to work on defense in the backcourt. The mid line and back line are combined to work on stopping the offense when they break the press and are going for the score. Lastly, all five are brought together to practice team defense in the full-court press.

Offense is no different; all parts of a play must be practiced, and that includes shooting. No matter how well a team executes team offense, someone must put the ball in the basket. We encourage coaches to include a healthy balance of game shooting in the practice plan. We equally encourage players to spend plenty of time shooting outside of practice. All the great ones did.

CHAPTER 9

Inside Moves

As previously discussed, at the Big Man Camp, we teach the perimeter one-on-one moves first. One of the reasons for this is that when those tall fellows are in the post, I want them to think more like wing players. I have found that many of them are locked into one or two low-post moves. These players have never explored the possibilities that can arise from effectively reading the defense. At the wing, we teach players to read the defense and be creative. We want the same thing in the post; we want players to have a multitude of moves at their disposal.

For example, remember the reverse step and drive from the wing? Many players would never think of using this move in the post. But it works. A quick baseline drop step often draws the defense back, opening up the short jump shot. At a minimum, it creates space and gets the defender reacting. However, before we get into the wonderful world of low-post scoring, please review the information in chapter 6 about the principles of good receiving and the block and tuck method (see pages 61 to 63). A player can't score without catching the ball first. And please use the DVD while reading this chapter. Everything in this chapter is demonstrated there.

At this point, the players have already learned proper body position and movement to the ball. Therefore, we can proceed to the one-on-one moves knowing that the player is able to receive the basketball in an operable area using the jump stop (making either foot available as a pivot foot).

One-on-One From the Post

Defending a skilled post player is a difficult assignment. There is no way that one player can take away the baseline and the middle at the same time; one or the other will be open. The other side of the coin is that the offensive player must quickly read which is open and must react with the proper move to score.

Turning vision toward the play immediately after the catch and two-footed landing is the first step toward determining where the defense is playing—and consequently, the first step in determining what options are available. First, the player reads whether the defender is playing tight or giving space. Each possibility triggers a separate series of moves. Once that has been determined, the player reads whether the defender is taking away the middle or the baseline. Again, each of those possibilities triggers a series of moves and countermoves. In the following sections, we present low-post moves in two stages: moves when the defender is playing tight and moves when the defender is giving space. All moves will be presented from the right side of the key.

Moves When the Defense Is Playing Close

The offensive post player has come to a jump stop and is looking over the right shoulder to the play. The defender is playing close and slightly to the middle. This signals a series of baseline moves and countermoves.

Baseline Moves for Tight Defense

The following moves are specifically designed to either take advantage of space given on reception of the basketball or create space through footwork. Pay special attention to the little things that make the moves successful. For example, any fakes used must be convincing. Take a look at the move that is being faked. The fake should look exactly like the first part of that move.

Move 1—Baseline Power Move 1   When looking toward the play, the offensive player sees that the defender is playing close and on the high side. The offensive player reads that the baseline is open. With the back vertical and a low center of gravity, the player makes the pivot and takes a long step directly toward the area immediately beside the rim (but not under the backboard); the lead foot is pointing to the hoop (see figure 9.1).

The footwork necessary to make this move can be described as "step, hop, jump stop." The first step (the drop step toward the rim) is accompanied by a simultaneous two-handed dribble. This dribble is performed close to the floor so that it almost appears as if the player has simply touched the floor with the ball without releasing it. After the dribble,

Figure 9.1 The player takes a long step with the lead foot pointing toward the basket.

the player springs off the lead foot and comes to a jump stop in the spot just beside the rim. This "step, hop, jump stop" action is difficult to explain but can be clearly seen on the DVD.

As a general rule, contact works in favor of the offensive player; it seals the defense and disallows defensive reaction and countermovement. When a player is making the baseline power move, contact is even more important because it ensures that the offensive player maintains inside position. When taking the initial long step toward the basket, the offensive player contacts the defender's legs with the backside. And when executing the following hop and jump stop, the player moves into the defender to maintain that contact.

Move 2—Baseline Power Move 2 (Pump Fake) When a player is making a power move to the baseline, the defender may sometimes recover enough to be able to put pressure on the direct layup. If so, a pump fake is needed to either freeze the defender or cause that defender to leave the feet.

The idea of a fake implies that the offensive player is deceiving the defender into thinking the shot will be taken. That means the fake must be convincing. Any action other than what is involved in the actual shot will hinder that deception. Therefore, when faking the layup, the player flexes the knees, moves the upper body slightly upward, and moves the ball up to, but no higher than, the eyebrows.

After a fake of any kind—in any situation and from any area of the floor—immediate counteraction is necessary. For that reason, especially when under the basket with the ball, the pump fake should be executed with no change in the center of gravity; the legs remain bent so that the shot can immediately follow the fake. In other words, for the actual shot, there is no need to lower the center of gravity again to coil the knees.

After the fake of a direct layup, the appropriate counteraction is the reverse layup. To avoid the traveling call, the player must jump off both feet (without moving either one) to reverse the ball.

Move 3—Fake Baseline Drop Step, Square Up, Jump Shot The baseline is open, and the offensive player begins the power move. However, the defender slides back and over to cut off the path. The offensive player counters with a step back, creating space for the jump shot (see figure 9.2).

Figure 9.2 The offensive player drop steps toward the baseline and is cut off by the defender; therefore, the offensive player steps back and creates space for the shot.

Move 4—Middle Sweep and Drive After faking the drop step and squaring up, the offensive player reads that the defender is reacting quickly and is coming out to put pressure on the jump shot. The player fakes the jump shot, sweeps the ball from right to left—with the ball very close to the floor (see figure 9.3)—and drives to the middle for the layup.

Figure 9.3 After faking the jump shot, the player sweeps the ball from right to left.

Move 5—Middle Kiki 1   As the offensive player drives toward the middle, the defender retreats to cut off the driving lane. The player reacts by planting the right foot and springing back to create space for the jump shot (see figure 9.4). When springing back, the player must turn to square up to the basket when landing. This will help ensure high-percentage shooting.

Move 6—Middle Kiki 2   If the defender reacts well when the offensive player springs back for the Kiki 1 move, this triggers the countermove, the Kiki 2. The offensive post player reads that the defender is reacting and closing the gap created by the Kiki 1 move. To counter, the offensive player raises up the head as if beginning the jump shot and then dives low toward the basket for the layup. The entire move requires two dribbles: The first dribble takes the player back, away from the defender, and the second dribble should be past the defender and toward the basket.

Move 7—Baseline Step Hook Shot   If the defense is giving the baseline but is not playing tight, the baseline step hook is available. The step directly toward the baseline creates the space necessary to get this shot off.

Figure 9.4   Middle Kiki 1: The offensive player springs back off the right foot after the defender has cut off the driving lane.

The accuracy of this shot is dependent on some very important details. Chapter 8 explains the importance of turning the stepping foot in the intended direction in order to release the hips. This allows the hips to rotate, freeing the upper body to rotate as well. The upper rotation permits the head to turn and look at the target. It also frees the shooting arm to follow through in the direction of the basket. In other words, a chain reaction is initiated with proper footwork—the rotation of the stepping foot. At the completion of the shot, if all is done right, the shooter will be facing the target, ready to move to the offensive rebound.

Figure 9.5 The baseline jump hook shot.

Move 8—Baseline Jump Hook Some players seem to be very effective with the jump hook, which is executed off two feet rather than one foot as required for the hook shot used in the previous move. This shot has become the most used post shot in today's professional game. The player begins in the crouched position, looking across the key toward the play. After reading that the baseline is open, the player steps toward the baseline, again releasing the hip to rotate, hops off that foot into a two-footed jump stop, and releases the jump hook (see figure 9.5; also refer to the DVD). The ending position is identical to that of the hook shot in the previous move; the player is facing the basket and should move toward the possible rebound.

Move 9—Baseline Spin Move As mentioned, the post player should look at the play when receiving the basketball; however, there is one exception—when the defender is playing very aggressively, physically pushing the back of the offensive player, on the high side. In this situation, the offensive player must keep the back vertical and the center of gravity low.

The idea is to make the defensive pressure work against the defender by releasing it. The offensive player spins the body 180 degrees and literally falls toward the basket with the upper body, while dribbling the ball with the hand away from the defender. The baseline foot is used as the pivot foot, and the outside foot comes completely around to step toward

Figure 9.6 The player spins toward the baseline. The baseline foot is the pivot foot, and the outside leg spins around and comes toward the basket.

the hoop (see figure 9.6). The dribble is made with the outside hand (away from the defender) in order to protect the ball and is immediately picked up with both hands. This action is followed by a hop off the lead foot and a jump stop beside the basket. A clear demonstration of this move is found on the DVD.

Middle Moves for Tight Defense

The offensive player has received the basketball at the mid-post area. The player reads the defense and sees that the defender is playing close and taking away the baseline. The middle is open.

Move 1—Hook Shot The player takes a long step, parallel to the baseline, and points the lead foot at the opposite sideline, opening up the hips. This movement starts the chain reaction that leads to the release of the shooting arm and a position facing the basket (see figure 9.7).

Figure 9.7 The player is in position for the hook shot.

Figure 9.8 The player is spinning toward the baseline.

Figure 9.9 After faking the shot, the player protects the ball and steps through to the basket.

Move 2—Jump Hook The one-footed step and jump for the hook shot leaves a player vulnerable to being thrown off line by physical contact. Against physical players who are capable of pushing the offensive player and causing a step away from the basket, the jump hook may be a more effective option. The offensive player takes one step, comes to a jump stop, and shoots the jump hook off both feet. This move allows the player to maintain a low center of gravity until the shot is initiated.

Move 3—Middle Reverse At times, when the offensive player is stepping into the key for the hook shot or jump hook, the defender may slide over to cut the player off. The countermove for this involves reversing direction by spinning toward the baseline immediately after the dribble is taken (see figure 9.8). Quick spinning in the direction of the basket is dependent on maintaining a low center of gravity and keeping the back in a vertical position.

Move 4—Middle McHale, Up and Under Although this move is used by many players at all levels, it is named for Kevin McHale, the great Boston Celtic of the 1980s, who perfected it. When making the move into the middle, instead of spinning baseline when the defender moved over, Kevin would step through, directly to the basket. This move is also known as the "up-and-under" move (see figure 9.9).

The player steps into the key with the intention of shooting the hook shot or jump hook, but the defender moves over and closes in. The player picks up the dribble, fakes the shot, and steps across and by the feet of the defender, toward the basket.

Although, technically, a one-footed step, lift, and one-footed takeoff for the shot is not a violation (because the pivot foot does not lift and land before the release of the shot), it is safer to finish the shot by jumping off both feet, as shown on the DVD.

Moves When the Defense Is Giving Space

All the post moves presented so far are based on reacting when the defender is playing close behind the offensive post player. In almost all instances, for the offensive player to create the space needed to shoot, the player threatened the drive to the basket, moving the defender back. Now let's look at some post moves for when the defender is giving space at reception. A defender may give space for various reasons. For example, a defender may give space if the offensive player has great power moves and hook shots. Another reason may be that the defender is not convinced that the offensive player can make the turnaround jump shot. Again, while providing space, the defender must choose whether to take away the baseline or the middle.

Baseline Moves for Loose Defense

Because the defender is playing back, space is already provided. But the offensive player can create more space by using the Sikma 1 move and then the Sikma 2 move as a counter.

Move 1—Sikma 1   The Seattle Supersonics' 1976 starting lineup was, comparatively, not tall. The center was Jack Sikma at 6 feet, 10 inches (just over 2 meters). Though small for a center, Jack presented plenty of challenges for defenders of all sizes. Like Kareem Abdul-Jabbar, Jack had one strong move and one counter, another testimony to the concept that a player does not need a plethora of offensive moves and counters to be effective. However, the strong move must be one that poses a serious threat for the defense. Sikma had such a move—a turnaround jump shot.

While keeping the basketball above his head, Jack made an inside pivot toward the baseline and faced the basket (see figure 9.10*a*). If the defender left any amount of space, Jack needed little body motion to get the jump shot off, and his slight fadeaway created even more space (see figure 9.10*b*).

Move 2—Sikma 2   If the defender closed in when Jack made his reverse turn to the baseline, Jack countered by faking the shot and driving past the defender and into the middle of the key for the short hook or jump shot (see figure 9.11).

Figure 9.10 Sikma 1 move: *(a)* reverse pivot with the ball overhead and *(b)* shooting the jump shot while fading away from the defender.

Figure 9.11 Sikma 2 move: driving past the defender after faking a turnaround jump shot.

Middle Moves for Loose Defense

The offensive player receives the ball, looks over the shoulder, and reads the defense. The defender is playing loose and taking away the baseline. The hook shot across the middle may work here, but the player must be careful not to be enticed into a charge; some defenders play loose—inviting offensive players to drop step, spin, or go across the key—so that the defender can step over to take the charge. Players can use the following moves to make the defender pay for allowing space.

Move 1—Back Pivot to Jump Shot   While back pivoting and squaring to the basket, the offensive player reads that the defender is not coming out. The player takes a quick jump shot, banking it off the backboard (figure 9.12). Shooting the ball "by" rather than "over" a defender requires quickness and deception. The closer to the basket, the more important that concept becomes. As the player turns to make the back pivot, he must maintain a low center of gravity so the threat of a drive is possible. The player must be able to release the jump shot at any time during the move; the goal is to shoot when the defender is most off balance or is farthest away. In other words, a full turn is not required.

Move 2—Back Pivot to Sweep and Drive   If the defender moves out to stop the jump shot, the offensive player fakes the shot, sweeps the ball low from right to left, and drives to the basket with a long step (see figure 9.13). To ensure a direct path to the basket and help seal the defender

Figure 9.12   Back pivot to jump shot.

Figure 9.13   After the shot fake, the player sweeps the ball low and drives to the basket with a long step.

from being able to recover, the offensive player makes contact with the defender's right side.

Move 3—Sweep to Kiki 1   If the defender recovers to stop the drive, the player plants the right foot and springs back for the Kiki 1 move (described earlier in this chapter).

Move 4—Sweep to Kiki 2   If the defender closes in when the player uses the Kiki 1 move, the player counters with the Kiki 2 move (described earlier in this chapter).

One-on-One From the High Post

The ultimate goal of the Big Man Camp is for players to be able to execute one-on-one moves in a live three-on-three situation on one side of the floor. We start with one-on-one moves at the wing, and then bring similar footwork into the mid post. Finally, we teach one-on-one play from the high post, particularly the elbow area. The combination of those three spots constitutes a strong-side triangle, an alignment found in almost every offense. We teach eight moves from the high post.

Move 1—Drop Step Layup   The ball is at the strong-side wing. Coming from the low-post area on the weak side, the offensive player makes a baseline fake, drawing the defense down, and cuts directly to the strong-side elbow area. The player receives the basketball with a two-footed jump stop, facing the intersection of the strong-side sideline and the half-court line (see figure 9.14a). If the defender is playing close at

Figure 9.14   The offensive player *(a)* receives the ball and comes to a jump stop; if the defender is close, the player *(b)* drops the left leg toward basket.

reception (most likely on the strong side), the player drops the left leg toward the basket and drives to the basket (see figure 9.14*b*).

Move 2—Drop Step Pull-Back Shot   When the offensive player begins the drop step, the defender reacts and drops back to cut off the drive. The offensive player creates space by pulling back, squares up to the basket, and takes the jump shot (see figure 9.15).

Move 3—Drop Step Rocker   As the player pulls back for the jump shot, the defender reacts and closes the gap, preventing the jump shot. The defender is approaching the left side of the player, leaving the middle open. The offensive player reacts by faking back and then using a rocker step toward the basket for the drive (see figure 9.16).

Move 4—Drop Step and Swing Through   As the offensive player pulls back from the drop step, this time the defender recovers toward the player's right side, leaving the left side open. The player counters by swinging the ball close to the floor from right to left and then driving to the basket, initiating contact with the defender on the way (see figure 9.17).

Figure 9.15   The offensive player pulls back after drop stepping.

Figure 9.16   The offensive player fakes back and then takes a rocker step.

Figure 9.17 The player swings the ball close to the floor.

Move 5—Kiki 1 Middle When receiving the ball, the offensive player either drop steps or pivots, depending on how close the defender is playing. When practicing these moves, the player should mix up drop steps and pivots.

The player drives to the basket, following a drop step or square up, and the defender reacts by retreating and cutting off the path. The player counters by using the Kiki 1 move (as previously described).

Move 6—Kiki 2 Middle The Kiki 2 move (previously described) is used when the defender reacts to the Kiki 1 move by closing in and putting pressure on the jump shot.

Move 7—Kiki 1 Baseline This move is only possible if no player is present at the strong-side low post. The player drives down the side of the free throw lane, and the defender reacts by dropping back. The offensive player counters by springing back to create space for the jump shot (as previously described).

Move 8—Kiki 2 Baseline The Kiki 2 move is used when the defender moves out with the offensive player who has executed the Kiki 1 move. As the defender comes, the player dives to the basket with a one-dribble drive for the score (as previously described).

Great Players With Great Moves

A lot of information, right? Too many moves? Yes, the previous moves are too many for any one player. It would take years to learn all of them. A complete, unstoppable low-post arsenal requires less moves than one may think. We can learn something from the greatest offensive player in the history of the NBA. He had one main move and one counter.

Kareem Abdul-Jabbar scored more points than anyone in professional basketball history. His main weapon was called "the sky hook." Once he was in motion for the sky hook, there was nothing for the defense to do but pray he was going to miss. But a miss was rare. More of a flip shot with the wrist rather than a true hook shot, the greatest single offensive weapon in basketball history was so effective that only one countermove was necessary.

On the left side, the countermove was a drop step to the baseline for the layup. On the right side, Kareem's main weapon was the baseline hook shot with the countermove being a left-handed hook shot across the key.

A common thread is found when examining the primary moves of great offensive centers. Each primary move creates space to shoot. Kareem opened space for the hook

Arguably the greatest weapon in basketball: Kareem Abdul-Jabbar's "sky hook."

shot with a fake the other way, a long step, and quick and substantial elevation. That space drew defenders and opened up countermoves.

Today, Tim Duncan is the most effective low-post offensive player in the NBA. The jump hook shot is his primary weapon. Because Tim plays basketball in perfect body position, he can elevate quickly. Keeping the legs bent and the back straight is the key to his ability to rise quickly for the jump hook. That quickness serves as a great fake, and because Duncan remains in balance, he can counter quickly. Tim's countermoves are usually layups.

Conclusion

Especially at the high school level, when at all possible, tall players should be included in drills that teach play from the wing spot—and sometimes the guard spot. There are many reasons for this. One, it's enjoyable. The big players love handling the ball and making moves from the perimeter. Who can forget Shaquille O'Neal in the 2007 NBA All-Star Game going one on one from the key? Two, high school post players will become forwards in college. Working on perimeter skills prepares them for the next level.

Likewise, the smaller players should practice post play. By including them in low-post drills, the coach may discover that a player has a hidden talent and may post up that player in games. Also, some players grow after high school, or they fill out. With post skills already intact, they may be well prepared to be used in the post in college.

CHAPTER 10

Screening

Screening was invented very early in basketball's history. In the beginning years, all defenses were man-to-man. Centers were average in size and played mostly at the high post. The ball was passed to the center, and the remaining four players moved around the perimeter (e.g., weaving). As the perimeter players interchanged, they looked for openings to cut to the basket and receive a pass from the center for a layup.

But defense quickly became more sophisticated through the use of sagging and especially switching, making it difficult for offensive players to get open and score. The screen delayed the switch because of the physical contact. In fact, for quite some time after the invention of screening, no rules governed the tactic. It was not unusual to see screens so aggressive that the defender was knocked down—and sometimes out. However, to prevent the "noncontact" sport of basketball from becoming too much like rugby or football, rules were instituted for screening. Because of screening, zone defense was invented. It took basketball coaches years to learn how to screen against zones, and even today, many still do not know how.

During discussions of zone offense at basketball camps, the question is often asked, "Should I teach my players to screen against zone defense?" The answer is "Not only *should* you screen against zone defense, you had *better* screen against zone defense." Man-to-man defenses are susceptible to one-on-one play without screening. The zone is not nearly as vulnerable. Therefore, openings must be created through devices that move zone defenders out of—or to the limit of—their zone areas. For example, the middle baseline defender in a 2-3 zone can be moved toward the free throw line, opening up the area under the basket. This can be done by using a cutter in the high-post area or simply by having the inside offensive player screen that defender up toward the free throw line (literally pushing the defender away from the basket).

Screening remains the most effective means for creating openings and penetrating both man-to-man and zone defenses. For example, the ball screen will create a momentary opening for one of the two engaged players, or it may cause a switch that leads to a mismatch. Furthermore, when the ball screen play penetrates the defense—either with the ball handler on the dribble or the screener on a roll—defensive help is required, which distorts the team defense. When this occurs, smart offensive players will move the ball to find the open player.

For man-to-man play, we cover four types of screens—the ball screen, the down screen, the cross-lane screen, and the back screen. In this chapter, we present the technical components of each type of screen. In chapter 11, we will show what makes each screening "play" effective. But before we get into those technical details for each screen, let's look at some screening principles that apply to all screens.

General Principles for Screening

Each type of screen has its own principles, but some general screening principles apply to all screens. Offensive players must keep the following principles in mind when involved in any screening play.

Screeners Must Become "Big" "Big" does not mean tall. Height is no advantage for screening. The screener must become as wide as possible while avoiding elbow contact with the cutter's defender. This is accomplished by bending the knees while keeping the upper body vertical and placing the hands on the knees. The feet should be a little wider than the shoulders for balance and width. The posture used most often has the screener folding the hands above the crotch area. The purpose is to get the elbows out of the way and avoid the foul. Placing the hands on the knees and tucking the elbows in so they make contact with the waist accomplishes the same thing, and this position provides more width because the upper arms remain on the side of the body (see figure 10.1).

Screeners Must Watch Their Own Defenders and Look to Score Watching the defender who is guarding the ball handler or cutter does the screener absolutely no good. When a screener watches his own defender, he will see opportunities to get open, receive the pass, and score. This dimension of screening action not only adds a second scorer, but also helps the cutter get open.

Cutters Are Responsible for Getting Open Getting big and watching his own defender for opportunities to get open are the only responsibilities in the job description of the screener. Although the screener gets low and

Figure 10.1 The screener becoming "big"—in a wide stance.

wide, providing maximum square footage to hinder the progress of the cutter's defender, it is the sole responsibility of the cutter to get open. If the coach does not make this clear, the following two ramifications will occur: (1) The screener will lean forward or sideways, setting a moving screen, and (2) the screener's attention will be drawn away from the priority—watching her own defender. Also, I have always taught that, prior to the screen, the offensive player with the ball fakes movement away from the screen. This may freeze the defender and help eliminate a screen on a quickly-moving defender.

Screeners Must Initiate Contact After the Screen One of the things we stress most at the Big Man Camp is that screeners should initiate contact with their own defender after the screen and should seal the defender (if a slip screen or roll is not used). If defenders are allowed to begin a move to get back into position after the screen, they are usually able to get that position. On the contrary, a first "hit" by the screener creates momentary space and, consequently, an opening. The moment the cutter's defender can no longer be screened, the screener should move into his own defender and create an opening at the low-post block area (see figure 10.2). A bounce pass with the baseline hand is the best method for getting the ball to the screener.

Figure 10.2 The screener creating an opening at the low-post block.

Ball Screen

A screen for the ball handler has been part of basketball for decades. However, at no time has it been more popular than in the present day. Every NBA team makes use of the ball screen, and many use it as the primary means of attack. Even Phil Jackson and Tex Winter, presently head and assistant coaches for the Los Angeles Lakers, have added the ball screen to their triangle offense. In the past, this offensive play was used almost exclusively by professional teams, but now it has filtered into college, high school, and international basketball. The ball screen is arguably the most effective team offensive weapon in modern basketball—domestic and international. Why? What's so good about the ball screen?

Penetrating a defense with the basketball is the key to creating defensive distortion and therefore adjustments—and is the key to creating offensive openings. The ball screen can effectively provide this penetration in two ways: A ball handler may turn the corner and dribble into the heart of the defense, or a screener may roll to the basket for the reception. Skilled and experienced offensive duos can create high-percentage shots almost every time the play is run. Defenders must often provide help in order to try to stop offensive penetration. As a result, offensive adjustments by the other three offensive players can manufacture alternative high-percentage shots when the ball is moved to the open player. Effective two-person ball screening involves three key principles.

Screeners Should Approach the Screen at a 90-Degree Angle

For a ball screen to work, the offensive players must cause the ball handler's defender to react by adjusting his position. The person guarding the dribbler should be forced to either drop below the screen to get through, move above the screen, or call for the switch. To cause this defender to have to make this choice, the screen must be set so that the line of the screener's shoulders is at a 90-degree angle to the path of the dribbler when coming off the screen.

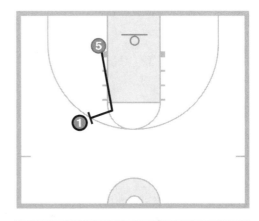

Figure 10.3 The path of the screener from the low post to the screen.

For example, when the ball handler is at the guard position on the left side, a screener coming from the low post should approach the screening area by moving straight up the side of the free throw lane to the elbow; the screener then turns and moves toward the ball handler at a sharp right angle (see figure 10.3). This ensures the correct angle.

Ball Handlers Are Responsible for Getting Open

Although this principle applies to all screens, it must be emphasized here because more moving screen violations occur for the ball screen than for any other type. If the ball handler and the screener both understand that all of the responsibility for getting open falls on the ball handler, ball screening will be more effective. The screener's job is to "set" the screen by remaining stationary. It is the ball handler's job to use the screen to lose the defender and get open. This understanding will help the screener avoid a moving screen violation.

Screeners Must Watch Their Own Defenders

When a screener knows that it is not his responsibility to get the ball handler open, this frees him to concentrate on his own defender. The moment that the defender moves to help on the dribbling ball handler, the screener can move to an open spot to receive the basketball (see figure 10.4).

Figure 10.4   The screener rolling to the basket.

Down Screen

The down screen is a two-player interchange where the wing player moves down toward the key to set a screen and free up a teammate who is already there. A down screen is often used with the goal of allowing the cutter to come off the screen to the perimeter for an open jump shot. However, more options are available (these options are detailed in chapter 11). The more options a duo exploits, the more effective down screening will be. In other words, the screener and cutter should strive to become skilled at reading the defense and using several options to take advantage of what the defense gives them. If the offensive players use only one or two options, the defense will be able to anticipate those moves and get into proper position to stop them.

Some screening principles apply to all types of screens. For example, the screener should make the move to get open when that opening occurs, even if it's before the interchange. Screeners should watch their own defenders. Cutters are responsible for getting open. In addition, the following key principles should be applied for the down screen.

Screeners Should Set the Screen Away From the Key

The traditional down screen was usually set with a single goal in mind—to get the cutter open on the perimeter. Therefore, in a traditional down screen, the screener would set the screen on the side of the free throw lane. Throughout basketball history, whenever a new offensive tactic is invented, defenses quickly learn to adjust. In the case of the down screen, defenders learned to anticipate the cut to the perimeter and learned to position themselves (i.e., play on top of the screen) to move out with the cutter, cutting off the pass. This was possible because the screen was being set so close to the basket that the threat of the backdoor cut was not an option. Moving the screen about two feet (.6 meter) out and away from the side of the free throw lane—at a 45-degree angle to the basket (see figure 10.5)—adds the backdoor option and leaves enough room for the cut to the perimeter. In the diagram, notice that the 45-degree line intersects with the side of the free throw lane above the block.

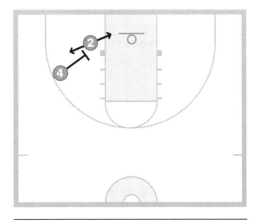

Figure 10.5 The screen is at a 45-degree angle to the basket.

Screeners Are Scorers

Especially against switching and hedging defenses, the screener should be considered a primary target. When defenders who are guarding screeners participate in helping teammates who are guarding cutters, an opening for the screener always occurs, though momentarily. Inexperienced players usually miss the opportunity. On the DVD and in chapter 11, we cover the various options for the down screen. In each option, the screener, if alert, has the opportunity to get open.

Moving the down screen two feet (.6 meter) farther away from the basket (see the previous principle) makes the slip screen cut into the key more effective than when closer in. The reason is that the ball handler has more time to pass. Open slip screeners are often missed because they get open so quickly.

The effectiveness of the down screen is dependent on the screener's scoring mentality. The screener must look for openings to receive the basketball by slipping the screen before the cutter uses it or by moving to an open spot after the screen. At a minimum, this keeps the defender busy and eliminates any help that defender can give to a teammate who is guarding the cutter.

Cutters Should Set the Defender Up

Because the screen is set a little farther away from the basket—adding the backdoor option for the cutter—that cutter is in great position to set up the defender. If the defender guarding the cutter is playing below the screen, a fake cut to the basket will draw the defender back, allowing the cutter to use the screen to lose that defender. If the defender is playing higher (above the screen or between players), anticipating the cut out, the cutter sets that defender up by making a fake cut toward the perimeter and then makes a backdoor cut if available.

Cutters and Screeners Should Make Contact

With the exception of the slip screen, the cutter should always make contact with the screener before attempting to get free from the defender. In fact, getting free is contingent on shutting down the space between the cutter and screener—space the cutter's defender can use to get through.

When coming off the screen, the cutter should be low; the cutter's inside shoulder should make contact with the screener's waist (figure 10.6).

Figure 10.6 The cutter makes shoulder contact with the screener's waist.

Cross-Lane or Lateral Screen

The cross-lane screen—also known as the *lateral screen*—involves a strong-side post player moving away from the ball (on the wing) to set a screen for the opposite post player, who comes to the strong-side block. For effective cross-lane screening, players must learn the following key principles.

Screeners Should Set the Screen Halfway Up the Key

The most common mistake in the execution of the cross-lane screen is the player interchange occurring too close to the basket, which eliminates the lob option. On the down screen and cross-lane screen, the basket area must remain open or it becomes easier to defend. When the possibility of the lob pass is added, this forces the cutter's defender to stay below the screen, making it easier for the cutter to get open coming over the top (figure 10.7).

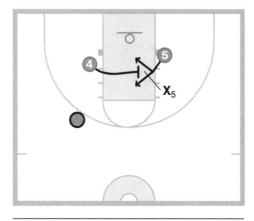

Figure 10.7 The cutter gets open coming over the top.

Screeners Should Set the Screen Halfway Across the Key

The screen must be set at least halfway across the key, close to the outside of the lane if possible. This helps avoid a three-second call and gives the cutter room to get the ball in a scoring area. Also, the cutter must wait to initiate the move in order to avoid a moving screen violation. The traditional cross-lane screen has the screener setting the screen near the middle of the key. Teams are moving away from that concept for the reasons just described. Setting the screen outside the lane still poses challenges for the defense. The cutter is more likely to be open earlier, closer to the basket. The screener can still come back to the elbow to create the triangle.

Cutters Should Move Away From the Screener

When the screener approaches, the cutter moves away from the screener and the ball. This ensures that the screener sets the screen at least halfway across the key, and it sets up the defender to be screened (figure 10.8).

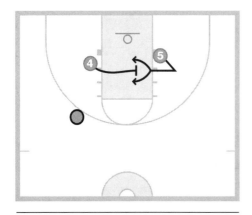

Figure 10.8 The cutter moves away from the screener.

Figure 10.9 The cutter cuts below the screen, and the screener moves to the high post.

Screeners and Cutters Should Separate

As soon as the cutter makes his move (chapter 11 presents all possible options), the cutter and screener quickly separate. The space created will expose any defensive error and will allow the passer to get the ball to the player with the greatest advantage. For example, if the cutter cuts below the screen (to the baseline side), the screener moves to the high-post area (see figure 10.9).

Back Screen

A back screen is a two-player maneuver where the player at the low post comes out to screen for a perimeter player. At the Big Man Camp, we do not use the back screen. Therefore, no explanation or demonstration is included in chapter 11 or the DVD. The back screen is highly used today, particularly in five-man motion and flex offenses. It is the primary means of creating openings in the flex offense. The back screen is a dangerous offensive maneuver for the defense because the cutter presents an immediate inside scoring threat and the screener is often open for the jump shot after the screen. Players must know the following two principles for the back screen.

Screeners Must Face the Key

Old-fashioned? Yes, we do not see players screening with their backs to their teammates today. As effective as it was, the UCLA cut (which originated in John Wooden's high-post offense) is not operated with the center facing the basket today. Why? I haven't got a clue. It seemed that at least once per game, the center would slip to the basket before the high-post screen and get an uncontested layup. That is not possible with the screener facing away from the hoop. Also, when a screener has his back to the cutter, it is difficult for him to commit a moving screen violation. For the back screen, the reasons the screener should face the basket are the same.

Cutters Must Accelerate

For either player to get open, the cutter must set the defender up by making a basket cut to either side of the screener and then accelerating away from the defender and straight to the basket. When making the basket cut, the cutter should literally touch the screener's back, closing the gap for the defender.

Conclusion

Many factors have changed the game at the college and high school levels in the past decades. One of the most important changes in the interpretation of a rule came about in the early 1970s. The legal screening position changed from three feet (.9 meter) away from the defender to a position directly on the defender. No one had any idea of the eventual ramifications that this seemingly simple change would bring about in the game. One of the essential duties in coaching is to clearly and deeply analyze any change in a rule or interpretation. A coach should always examine the rule and evaluate how he or she can best adjust to it. In the past, if coaches did not like a rule change, some would give the new rule little thought and would dismiss the change with, "I'm not going to change." Some of these coaches never adjusted and have never had much success with their teams.

One coach who did examine the new interpretation of the screening rule was Bobby Knight of Indiana University. He adjusted his offensive scheme of play to make the best use of the new interpretation. At a very early age, Coach Knight had gained prominence in the coaching fraternity as a coach with a marvelous future ahead of him. Previously, he had adopted an offense called *reverse action* that best suited his personnel at West Point, where he had great success with his basketball program. Indiana University had made a coaching change and picked Coach Knight as the next basketball coach. Indiana was one of the most highly respected basketball programs in the college ranks and had a great history of success. The style of basketball at Indiana was distinctly different from what was needed at West Point. The personnel at Indiana were a higher caliber of player. The Indiana Hoosiers were known nationally as the "Hurryin' Hoosiers," and their team lived up to that name. The change in the screening rule caused Coach Knight to adjust his offensive concepts. The rest is history.

I must add that Coach Knight began his offense from a two-guard front, and he initiates his half-court offense the same today. Taking full advantage of the screening rule change, Coach Knight designed a five-man offense with incessant back screening and down screening. He called this new system *motion offense*. Each time the basketball was returned to the top of the key, players on both sides of the lane set aggressive screens and used them to look for layups and open jump shots. Never before had defenses faced such an onslaught of screens. And Coach Knight's players were trained to have the patience to wait for the highest-percentage situation. Time and again, his players would make uncontested layups and wide-open jump shots. Today, motion offense (in various forms) is the most used offensive system at the high school level.

CHAPTER 11

Two- and Three-Player Plays

One-on-one play is one dimensional in that only one mind is involved: that of the offensive player. On reception of the basketball, players read the defense and react. When making the move, the same happens. However, when we add another offensive and defensive player, creating two-on-two basketball, things change. Executing a one-on-one play becomes more difficult because another defender is present and can help. Add another set of players, making it a three-on-three situation, and the difficulty again increases. Spacing is now an issue because offensive players have less room to operate.

Team basketball is vastly different from one-on-one. Because more players are protecting the basket, openings to penetrate the defense must be created through *plays*. Plays involve two or more players using offensive tactics—screening, cutting, options, and reading the defense—to move defensive players out of position between their assignments and the basket. Offensive plays are designed to cause defensive movement that creates momentary openings and advantages, either inside or out. Execution of a play is considered good when the offense creates an opening and gets the ball to a player in a high-percentage scoring position.

Basketball is a game of counters. For one-on-one basketball, we have discussed counters for every defensive action. In this chapter, we present two-on-two and three-on-three plays. Again, plays and counterplays are presented so players can learn to read the defense and take advantage of scoring opportunities.

Two-on-Two

We begin with two-on-two play, first discussing how to get the ball into the post when that player is facing pass denial pressure on the high or low side. Next, we cover passing the ball directly into a post player who is open (against soft defense). Finally, we explain the different options when using the ball screen and the down screen.

Two-on-Two Against Tight, Three-Quarter, Baseline and Middle Pressure

At times, a direct pass into the post is a low-percentage play because the post defender is playing tight defense on the high or low side of the post player. This makes the defender a threat to intercept or deflect the pass. In this situation, a change of angle is required. When the wing player with the ball sees that the defensive post player has stepped to the side of the post player and somewhat into the passing line, the wing reacts by dribbling toward the baseline or toward the top of the key to take the defender out of the line of the pass. However, to create a clear passing line, the post player must hold the defender and keep that defender from getting around.

Two-on-Two Against Tight, Three-Quarter, Baseline Pressure

We begin by placing all four players in a low-post stack. A *low-post stack* is created when the offensive post player straddles the first mark above the block and the wing player is stationed on the block. This initial positioning allows three important options: The wing player can use the post player as a screen and cut to the wing at a 45-degree angle; the wing player also has enough room to make a quick backdoor cut under the basket; and the post player can slip screen into the key using a cut that is parallel to the free throw line (see figure 11.1).

When the wing player cuts to the wing, the inside defender can play the post player several ways. We begin by teaching execution when the defender is playing denial defense on the baseline side (see figure 11.2a).

Seeing that the passing line is blocked, both offensive players work to create a new and

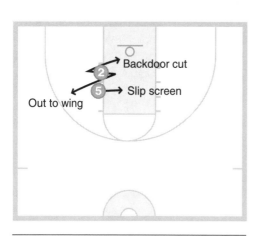

Figure 11.1   A low-post stack.

Figure 11.2 *(a)* The defender playing the post player on the baseline side. *(b)* The post player uses the back and arms and is about to step in front of the defender, keeping his opponent on the low side while the teammate dribbles toward the top of the key.

open passing line. The ball handler dribbles to the middle, while the low-post player seals the defender away from the basket by stepping across the feet and blocking the path to the key (see figure 11.2*b*).

When sealing, the post player initiates the contact and moves the defender even farther away from the hoop if possible. In other words, the post player is blocking the defender from the desired area of reception—somewhere inside the key. For effective sealing, the player's upper back should be as vertical as possible. A vertical back hinders defenders from placing a hand in the passing lane. The offensive post player's arms should be out to the side with the fingers facing the ceiling.

Timing is everything. When the ball handler takes the dribble to the middle to help create the angle, if the sealer leaves prematurely, the opening will close quickly. If the player leaves too late, the defender will recover into the passing line. A good rule of thumb is that it's better to leave too late than too early.

Two-on-Two Against Tight, Three-Quarter, Middle Pressure

In the same situation, the post defender is now playing on the high, or middle, side of the center. As the wing player takes one dribble toward the baseline, the post player steps in front of the defender, sealing that player from the baseline (see figure 11.3). A new passing line has been created. If the post player receives the basketball too close to the baseline, a layup may be difficult because the post player may be caught under the basket. For that reason, when sealing, the player must initiate the contact and move the defender even farther away from the baseline, if possible. Also, in this situation, the post player must wait until the pass is almost there. Leaving too soon will allow the defender to squeeze the post player under the basket.

Figure 11.3 The post seals the defender away from the baseline while the teammate creates a good passing angle.

Figure 11.4 The post player has good balance and presents an excellent target for the passer.

Two-on-Two Against Soft Defense

"Soft defense" refers to a defender playing behind the offensive post player and providing some space. In other words, the defender does not deny the pass (see figure 11.4). In this situation, the wing player delivers an overhead pass, and the post player catches the ball in the air, comes to a jump stop, and looks over the shoulder closest to mid court at the play. The player reads the defense and makes the appropriate move.

Four effective moves against loose defense were presented in chapter 9: Sikma 1, Sikma 2, sweep to Kiki 1, and sweep to Kiki 2.

Gamelike Application

A gamelike variation of the two-on-two wing and post drills is to have the post player come across the key to get open in the ball-side post. The post player should practice using all three of the ways to get open in this situation (as described in chapter 5). The two offensive players start by occupying both low-post positions. One comes out to the wing to receive the ball. Slightly after the wing player has made the move to the three-point line, the opposite post player cuts across the key to receive the ball (see figure 11.5). Timing is good when the post player is almost in position when the wing player receives the ball. The wing player can pass directly into the post if the player is open. If not, the wing player can use the dribble to the middle or to the baseline to create a better passing angle while the post player seals the defender.

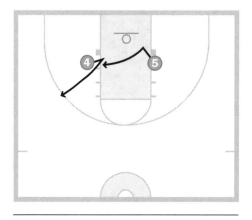

Figure 11.5 A wing player makes a move to the perimeter while the post cuts across the key.

As the post player is coming across the key, the wing player should be keeping the defender occupied by using the pivots and fakes described in chapter 5, such as the reverse pivot, the front pivot, and the drive fake. The passer should be in a triple-threat position—crouched with the ball around chest level. Standing with the ball above the head, ready to pass, only telegraphs the play and allows defenders to anticipate.

After the pass to the post, if the wing defender drops down to double-team inside, the wing player moves to a perimeter position that is the greatest distance from the defender who left for the double team; the wing player then looks for the return pass from the post player. For example, if the double team occurs on the baseline side of the post player, the wing player moves toward the center of the court (see figure 11.6). If the double team is on the high side, the baseline area is the greatest distance (see figure 11.7).

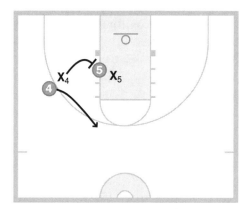

Figure 11.6 The wing player moves toward the center of the court to create maximum space.

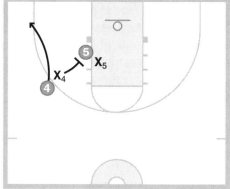

Figure 11.7 The wing player moves toward the baseline to create maximum space.

Ball Screen

At lower levels of basketball, where players are inexperienced, the ball screen often looks hurried and mechanical. In other words, time and again, the screen is set, the ball handler comes off the screen, and the screener rolls to the basket. However, at higher levels, a more varied approach can be seen. The screen is often set well away from the dribbler, allowing space for one-on-one execution and maneuvering to get the defender caught in the screen. Also, the offensive players read the defense throughout the play, and they react with a variety of moves to create space and openings.

We point this out because, although the options for ball screening are presented here, we encourage the coach to think of them as just that—options. Although we feel that the list is fairly complete and can answer most defensive methods of attack, other options will be discovered by players whose coaches encourage them to be creative and think outside the box. Those of us who have been around the block a few times know that the ball screen attack has as many options as the positions of the two defensive players throughout the play. And, believe me, that's a lot.

Options for the Ball Screen

With that said, let's look at four options for attacking with the ball screen: the jump shot, middle attack, outside attack, and slip screen. Offensive players determine which option to use based on how the defense plays the ball screen. Remember, reading the defense and reacting to get open are more important than going through the preconceived motions, or pattern, of a ball screen.

Jump Shot (No Switch)   The ball handler's quick and tight cut off the screen is usually the first move that will shift the defense and create openings. However, at times, that ball handler may be open for the jump shot right after coming off the screen (see figure 11.8).

Figure 11.8   The ball screen creates an open jump shot for the ball handler.

Middle Attack Switching defenses are designed to prevent penetration. However, against a ball screen, such a defense may be giving up just that. As the ball handler comes tightly off the screen and draws the screener's defender, the screener seals and rolls to the basket. Because of the looseness of the defense, there is often room to make the leading bounce pass between the players (see figure 11.9).

Outside Attack If the defense makes a tight switch (both defenders move in and are close to their new assignments), the ball handler dribbles laterally and makes a hook pass around the switching defender to the rolling screener (see figure 11.10).

Figure 11.9 The ball handler recognizes the defensive switch and passes the ball to the teammate who is rolling to the basket.

Figure 11.10 The ball handler makes a hook pass as the screener seals and holds the defender.

Because of the proximity of the defenders, when the screener rolls, the screener must initiate contact with the new defender and maintain that contact while awaiting the pass. The value of the screener initiating and holding contact cannot be overemphasized; it is the key to good execution. Also, the ball handler may need more than one dribble to create space for the hook pass.

Slip Screen   In the NBA, switching on a pick-and-roll is suicide because it creates size mismatches that will be exploited. On the other hand, providing no assistance will surely result in dribble penetration. The most used method in the NBA for rendering a ball screen ineffective is the "hedge and recover." As the ball handler dribbles off the screen, the screener's defender moves into the dribbler's path—diverting that player away from the basket—and then recovers to the original assignment.

In this situation, the slip screen (a quick, accelerated roll to the basket by the screener) can be very effective, because the hedging defender is counting on being able to recover. The moment the screener sees the initiation of the hedge, the screener makes the roll—whether this occurs before or after the ball handler has used the screen.

Since the screener has rolled early and increased the distance for the defender's recovery, this creates a problem for the defense. The proper pass to the rolling screener is a one-handed flip pass over the head of the defender (see figure 11.11).

Figure 11.11   The screener shows an excellent target as the ball is passed after the defensive switch.

Live Two-on-Two Ball Screen Practice

Going "live" implies that all previously presented options are available and should be employed when appropriate. Up to this point, the repetition of isolated options has been used to help players learn to read and react to various methods of guarding the ball screen. Now they must learn to read whatever the defense presents. This means errors will be made.

Therefore, live two-on-two must be a "controlled" activity. At the Big Man Camp, we stop the action every time an error occurs. More detail on teaching live activities is presented in chapter 15, but for now, the coach must know that it's important to draw attention to errors that hindered the effectiveness of the play. This encourages team play.

Coaches should anticipate errors and be ready to correct them. For example, in two-on-two play, the following errors are common: the post player incorrectly timing the turn and not getting open; the wing player not using one of the four options for getting open; the wing player failing to spot up after the ball is passed into the post and a double team has occurred; or the players not recognizing a loosely or tightly switching defense on the ball screen.

Producing a high-percentage shot quickly may not be possible. When the players realize they have not generated the shot they want, they should reset the play. This teaches patience and purpose. How do players recognize "the shot they want"? Before commencing play, the coach can identify where the potential high-percentage situations will be (for each combination of players). The best option could be a certain player in the low post or a great shooter on the wing or coming off the ball screen.

Down Screen

A down screen occurs when the wing player moves toward the basket at a 45-degree angle and sets a screen for a player already in that area. Preparation for the interchange is very important for proper execution and for making things as difficult as possible for the defenders. Like for the ball screen—and all screens for that matter—100 percent of the responsibility for getting open is placed on the player using the screen.

Options for the Down Screen

Options for the down screen include the backdoor cut, jump shot, curl, and flare. The cutter selects the appropriate option based on the route her defender takes to get around the screen.

Backdoor Cut   When the cutter is coming off the screen, defenders often anticipate and fight through the screen, staying even with the cutter. In this case, the cutter makes a hard cut under the basket, looking for the pass from the top (see figure 11.12). Because the screener's defender may drop to cover the pass, the screener is ready to cut up the lane and to the ball for the short jump shot.

Jump Shot When the cutter comes off the screen, the defender may get caught between the screen and the basket. In this case, the cutter comes out at about a 45-degree angle so that the screener is aligned between the defender and the cutter. This creates space for a perimeter jump shot (see figure 11.13). The screener watches for the switch or hedge and is ready to cut straight into the key for the reception and jump hook shot.

Figure 11.12 The first option of a down screen is the backdoor cut.

Figure 11.13 The cutter is able to get open on the wing, using the down screen.

Curl   All coaches have their favorite methods of guarding the down screen. Because of great outside shooting in the NBA, many coaches have the cutter's defender follow directly behind that cutter—this is called "shadowing the cutter." When done correctly, the defender becomes virtually impossible to screen.

When the cutter is shadowed by the defender while coming off the screen, the offensive cutter "curls" around the screener and straight into the key (see figure 11.14a). That player should be open unless the screener's defender steps out and blocks the path, in which case the screener pops into the key for the reception (see figure 11.14b).

Figure 11.14   (a) The cutter loses the defender by curling around the down screen. (b) Screeners can get open by following the curler.

Flare Some defensive systems direct the cutter's defender to fight between the screener and the screener's defender, who opens up to create space for the move through. Reading the defense, the cutter flattens out to the baseline and away from the basket in order to create space for the jump shot (see figure 11.15). Because the screener's defender has stepped back to open a gap for the teammate, the screener should be very alert to the opportunity to slip into the key for the reception. If that move is not available, the screener prepares to seal, as we will see in the final principle.

Figure 11.15 The cutter loses the defender in the screen and flares to the baseline to create maximum space.

Hit Seal Man

The myth about down screening is that the only objective is to get the cutter open for the jump shot. But that is only half the picture and presents only half the possibilities. The screener is always a potential receiver for a high-percentage situation. In fact, there may be more high-percentage scoring opportunities for the screener than for the cutter. When the cutter comes off the screen and stays close to the baseline, the screener has a wonderful opportunity.

Because the cutter made the "flat" cut, the defender was caught on the high side of the screen (see figure 11.16). In most cases, the screener's defender opened the gap and let the cutter's defender through. This

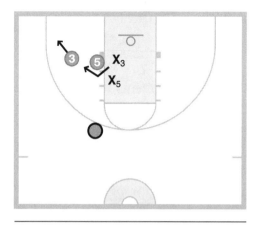

Figure 11.16 In order to create maximum space, the cutter flares to the corner when the defender is caught on the top side of the screen.

usually means that the screener is closer to the baseline than the defender is.

In this situation, the offensive player initiates contact and seals the defender to the high side, moving him higher if possible. The ball handler provides a pass away from the post defender and leads the post player to the basket for the layup.

Live Two-on-Two Combination

When the players have learned all the tactics that we've just discussed—sealing against baseline or middle pressure, receiving the ball at the low post against soft defense, and reading defenses against the ball screen and down screen—they are ready to operate in a live two-on-two situation where any and all of these tactics are possibilities. With a coach in possession of the ball at the guard spot, the wing player down screens, and the cutter comes to the wing to receive the ball. From there, that player can pass into the post—either directly or after using a dribble when tight middle or baseline pressure is being put on the center—or receive a ball screen. The coach must insist that the players only use the moves that have been taught. Other than individual one-on-one moves when open, no other maneuvers should be allowed.

If the wing player cannot get open, that player can set the down screen or cut to the basket and back out, using the methods learned for getting open. Any time the play is defended, the ball should be passed back out to the top, and the play should be reset.

Three-on-Three

Because of the success of Michael Jordan and the Chicago Bulls of the 1990s, the term *triangle offense* reemerged in basketball language. Tex Winter, the assistant coach, convinced Phil Jackson that the system would create one-on-one opportunities for all players, especially Jordan and Scottie Pippen, the team's two most prolific scorers. On the strong side, triangles were created with about 15-foot (4.5-meter) spacing between players, making the offense resistant to double teams.

At the Big Man Camp, we create a strong-side triangle by placing one player at the low post, one on the wing, and the third at the high post.

However, the high-post player begins at the weak-side block and comes to the strong-side elbow when needed to relieve the low-post player of defensive pressure that is denying the pass in from the wing.

For effective three-on-three play, we teach the low-post player how to seal the defender when the defense denies the pass in from the wing. We also teach the options for the cross-lane screen.

Low-Post Seal

After the initial down screen, bringing one player to the wing, the weak-side player watches the defender on the post player carefully. If the pass cannot be made into the post, the weak-side player reacts by cutting to the ball-side elbow of the key (see figure 11.17). The post defender denying the pass from the wing is preventing the pass from either the baseline side or the middle side of the post player.

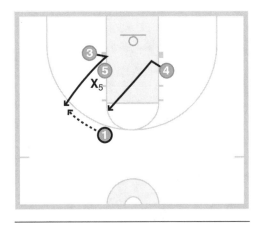

Figure 11.17 The weak-side player comes to the ball-side elbow to get the ball to the post player who is being pressured.

Post Defender Plays Low Side

If the defender is playing on the baseline side of the low-post player, the low-post player seals the defender away from the key by initiating and maintaining contact as long as possible (see figure 11.18). The high-post player delivers a leading bounce pass. The post player does not release

Figure 11.18 With the ball coming to the high post, the low-post player seals the defender away from the passing lane.

the seal until after the pass is made. Note that the high-post player, when receiving the ball, may make the quick reverse or take the jump shot if available. Remember, it is the players who make the plays. So, if the high-post player has a high-percentage move, that move should be made.

Figure 11.19 The post player makes a quick back pivot to seal the defender and get open for the pass from the high post.

Post Defender Plays High Side

Again, the weak-side player recognizes pass denial pressure on the post and comes to the high-post elbow. This time the post defender has denied the pass on the middle side. The post player seals the defender away from the key by making a quick back pivot, initiating and maintaining contact by lowering the center of gravity and keeping the upper back as vertical as possible (see figure 11.19). The post player's upper arms are parallel to the floor, and the hands are pointed up to the ceiling, ensuring a bigger area for the defender to get around.

Generally, the higher the offensive post player moves up the side of the lane, the less likely it is that the defender will front, because it becomes extremely uncomfortable for the defense. Conversely, the lower the offensive player goes, the more likely the front. Therefore, when being denied from the middle side, if the offensive player moves down the lane a foot (.3 meter) or so, the defender is very likely to make the complete front—and become even more vulnerable to the seal.

Cross-Lane Screen

A screen by the strong-side post player for a teammate on the opposite block can be very effective, not only in bringing the weak-side player to the strong-side post, but in getting the screener open as well. Traditionally, block-to-block screens have been executed with the players close to the basket. However, this makes things easier for the defense because the basket area is clogged. Moving the cross-lane screen to the mid post, or even higher, adds the threat of the immediate pass over the top for the layup. We teach players the following options for the cross-lane screen.

Middle Cut

The screener sets the screen, and the cutter's defender is attempting to avoid the screen by moving to the baseline side. The cutter makes the baseline fake, drawing the defender even lower, and then makes the middle cut (see figure 11.20*a*). Because the middle is open, the screener can slip the screen and take one step toward the ball for the pass and score (see figure 11.20*b*).

Figure 11.20 *(a)* With the defender on the low side of the screen, the cutter comes to the middle. *(b)* It can be argued that screeners are equally eligible as receivers.

Figure 11.21 The cutter takes the defender high and attempts to get open by cutting baseline.

Baseline Cut

If the cutter's defender chooses to play the high side, the cutter takes that defender even higher and then makes a sharp baseline cut off the screener (see figure 11.21). Again, the screener may be open the moment the cutter's defender fights through the screen.

Live Three-on-Three

When the players go three-on-three live, we're looking for three things: players using the strategies they've been taught to get open; proper execution and timing through the recognition of, and reaction to, offensive advantages in matchups or position; and players using the individual moves to score when available. Because we believe that team scoring is primarily dependent on players making individual plays, we reward one-on-one initiative, particularly if the moves used are ones practiced at camp. We encourage players to learn to recognize those individual opportunities.

A Dynamic Duo

When Karl Malone played for the Utah Jazz under the direction of Jerry Sloan, the success of the team was mostly credited to impeccable half-court offensive execution. The team also had an equally sound team defense that was well prepared to handle any play. The trademark of the team's offensive system was the "screen-and-roll" (pick-and-roll) operated almost exclusively by Malone and John Stockton. The difference in size between the two—Malone at 6 feet, 10 inches (208 centimeters), and 260 pounds (118 kilograms) and Stockton at 6 feet, 1 inch (185 centimeters), and 175 pounds (79 kilograms)—made defensive switching a serious liability to opponents. If Stockton kept the ball, dribble penetration was imminent, and if Malone rolled to the basket or posted, a score would most assuredly follow. Offensive execution is dependent on penetration, and the Malone and Stockton ball screen provided just that.

Karl Malone and John Stockton run the pick-and-roll.

Often called the "quintessential pick-and-roll duo," Stockton and Malone executed the screen-and-roll not only with precision but also with intelligent creativity. As previously discussed, there are limited ways to defend the screen-and-roll, each one with its own strengths and liabilities. When executing this play, Stockton and Malone almost never failed to instantly recognize the liability and capitalize on it. When John's defender was caught in a screen or jumped beyond the screen in anticipation, John quickly drove to the basket. When Malone's man helped on the screen—even for a moment—Karl was gone to the basket. When Malone's man dropped back too far, Karl popped out for the outside shot. Watching defenders attempt various methods of stopping the Stockton and Malone pick-and-roll was frankly rather sad. Time and again, the duo would come up with a high-percentage play.

Conclusion

The three-on-three play presented in this chapter is limited to the strong side only. Because of time constraints and the absence of guards at the Big Man Camp, that is all we can get to. Let this serve as an introduction to what is possible for practice sessions and for informal play ("pickup ball") in the off-season. For the coach, two-on-two and three-on-three strong side is an example of the effectiveness of breaking down an offense and adding players to come closer to five-on-five. By adding a fourth player at the top of the key, replacing the coach who has served as a passer to make the entry pass, the play can be reversed, and weak-side action can be added. For the player, why spend the summer playing helter-skelter basketball when you can improve as a team player? Get some players together who are willing to play positions and work on executing plays. This type of basketball still includes plenty of opportunity for one-on-one play.

CHAPTER 12

Post Play for All Positions

When Dr. Naismith invented basketball, the entire floor was divided into three distinct parts: the guard section (the third of the floor closest to the opponent's basket), the center section (the middle third of the floor), and the forward section (the third of the floor where players could score). Lines were drawn that players were not allowed to cross. As a result, players' roles were strictly defined by their location on the court.

Even after those lines were erased, players continued to have specific roles. Half-court offenses usually ran all plays through a player in the middle. That player received the basketball either at the high post or the mid post. After the pass, depending on the coach's system, perimeter players made backdoor cuts, placed screens, or interchanged through weaving. Those weaves were designed to create a defensive error, resulting in a cut to the basket for the layup or an outside shot.

Whatever the offensive pattern, early players were still confined to roles. The center was a passer and made an occasional move to score. The center never went out to the perimeter. Perimeter players remained on the outside and worked for basket cuts or jump shots. One guard was the point, and the other was the floor guard, or shooter.

In the 1970s, motion offense was introduced, primarily as a necessity. Title IX mandated that girls' and boys' basketball programs have equal gymnasium time. With limited hours of practice, teaching traditional offenses was nearly impossible. Those offensive systems were complex, and they required much more time and repetition for players to grasp and master them to a point where the players could execute them in games.

Motion offense, on the other hand, was much easier to teach and learn. It is a system that involves five players moving, screening, and cutting, leaving the middle open for backdoors and drives to the basket. This effectively eliminated the need for back-to-the-basket post players. The player who was prized in a motion offense (and on the defensive end against such an offense) was the jack-of-all-trades, the player who could handle the ball in space on the perimeter yet also maneuver successfully in traffic in the lane. The tall player who needed developing—with limited mobility and weak ballhandling skills—had a difficult time making the team, much less getting playing time. And coaches had little time to develop these big kids.

The absence of true back-to-the-basket players has led to what is called "dish and dunk" basketball. Teams run offenses that spread the floor, allowing for dribble penetration. When the dribble is stopped, the dish is made to a player on the perimeter, most often for a three-point shot. At the college and pro levels, those dribblers are looking to dunk when they penetrate.

But good coaches know that this type of offensive approach—if used exclusively—cannot consistently produce wins. As long as the game of basketball is played on the same-size court and with five players on each team, the team that controls the paint will almost always control the game. It is the balance of inside to outside basketball that produces scoring opportunities at multiple positions. When a team focuses on working the ball inside for the layup or easy inside move, this opens up the outside.

John Wooden says coaches and players would do well to remember the importance of getting the ball inside. Coach Wooden has made the following observation: "In today's game, it seems that players either want to shoot the three-point shot or dunk the basketball. The inside game has virtually vanished. What coaches may not know is that offensive basketball, in order to be consistently effective, must have an inside-out approach. By that I mean, generally speaking, the outside shot should come as a result of a defense dropping down to prevent the inside score. When a team has the opposite approach, working for an outside shot first, it is more difficult to get a high-percentage outside shot. I prefer to work off a player who has received the ball inside by cutting and moving. This frees outside shooters who may be able to get two or three feet (.6 or .9 meter) closer to the basket for the shot."

Versatility and Athleticism

The demise of the "true post player" was a negative consequence of motion offense. However, what the system did was create opportunities for all players who were skilled beyond traditional positions to assert themselves in the lane area. In just a few years, basketball fans began to witness players who could shoot the outside shot, dribble, penetrate, pass, and defend on the perimeter and in the post. And, at times, a particularly gifted tall player surfaced who could do all of those things.

The Magic Man

In the 1980 NBA finals, the Los Angeles Lakers held a lead of three games to two over the Philadelphia 76ers. The bad news was that the Lakers' great center, Kareem Abdul-Jabbar, could not play game 6 of the series in Philly. But the good news was that the Lakers did have Earvin Johnson Jr. At 6-foot-9 (206 centimeters) and playing point guard, the man known as "Magic" was the most versatile player basketball had ever seen. If anyone could fill the void left by Jabbar at the center position, it would be Magic.

From the time he first stepped on a court, Johnson amazed fans that a player of his size was able to do so much with the basketball. Several years previously, Oscar Robertson had established himself as the most versatile player the game had ever seen. "The Big O," as he was known, didn't merely record a triple double every now and then; he *averaged* double digits in points, rebounds, and assists over the course of an entire NBA season (and he averaged 25.7 points, 9.5 assists, and 7.5 rebounds during a 14-year pro career). But Magic was four inches (10 centimeters) taller than Oscar, and he was seemingly capable of doing anything on the court that he pleased—and always with that endearing smile.

NBAE/Getty Images

Standing six-foot-nine, Earvin "Magic" Johnson displayed exceptional ballhandling skill.

Johnson was first called "Magic" when he starred at Everett High School in Michigan. A sportswriter gave him that nickname after witnessing him dominate a game with 36 points, 16 rebounds, and 16 assists. That year, Magic led his team to the state championship with only one loss.

Johnson chose to stay close to home when making his college choice, joining Jud Heathcote's roster at Michigan State University. Johnson's impact on the program was immediate and enormous. In his first year, he led the Spartans to a Big Ten title and an appearance in the Elite Eight of the NCAA tournament (where Michigan State lost by 3 points to eventual champion Kentucky). As just a freshman, he averaged 17 points, 8 rebounds, and more than 7 assists a game. As a sophomore, he led the Spartans to the NCAA title, defeating Larry Bird's Indiana State Sycamores in the final game.

The next step was to conquer the NBA, and Johnson quickly demonstrated his "magic" to the Lakers and the rest of the league. Magic had a phenomenal rookie season—putting up double digits in scoring, rebounding, and assists in many games—and he made the triple double the new gold standard for outstanding performance.

So, in game 6 of the NBA finals that season, minus the ailing Jabbar, the Lakers had Magic Johnson jump center. And from there he played every position and proceeded to do whatever his team needed to win the game and the title. When he had a size advantage, he made mincemeat of smaller and weaker players, shooting turnaround jumpers, using drop steps, and making hooks. He came off ball screens and hit the outside jumper. He led the Lakers' famous "showtime" fast break, making passes that dazzled not only the crowd, but also his teammates. As his teammate Michael Cooper once said, "There have been times when he has thrown passes and I wasn't sure where he was going. Then one of our guys catches the ball and scores, and I run back up the floor convinced that he must've thrown it through somebody" (NBA.com).

In two seasons, Magic Johnson achieved much more than NCAA and NBA championships. During that brief blip on the screen of basketball history's time line, Magic verified that in the modern game, the labels of guard, forward, and center are position designations only—they are not defining terms regarding what, where, or how a player performs on the court.

Oscar Robertson, Magic Johnson, and Michael Jordan set the precedent and standard for versatile play that coaches and players seek today. The mechanical, one-dimensional player has become a thing of the past. Teams simply can't afford to put such players on the floor. A player who isn't a good shooter, for example, had better be a great rebounder, screener, defender, and passer. And simply being a deadeye shooter doesn't cut it unless the player can also guard effectively on the other end of the court.

Today we see extremely athletic players who can do wonderful things with the basketball. And they excel not just in one skill, but in several.

That's to take nothing away from the contributions of players such as Angelo "Hank" Luisetti, who in the late 1930s was the first to master the one-hand shot. At Stanford University, the 6-foot, 3-inch (75-centimeter) Luisetti became a phenomenon with his quick and accurate shot that opponents found impossible to stop. With that weapon in his arsenal, Luisetti became the first college player to score 50 points in a game and broke the national scoring record for a season. He led Stanford to an upset victory over Long Island University (breaking the Blackbirds' 43-game winning streak) and earned All-American honors.

We also can't diminish the contributions of players with amazing dribbling ability, such as Earl "The Pearl" Monroe, who could dazzle the crowd with his spinning, twisting, faking, and double-pumping repertoire of ballhandling skills. The Pearl was the ultimate playground player and was the first truly spectacular dribbler of the NBA, first with the Baltimore Bullets and then with the New York Knicks. Earl's lasting mark on the game of basketball was his introduction of a dribbling maneuver that no one had ever seen before. It was a 180-degree spin dribble with one hand. Those on the playgrounds called it the "Pearl dribble," and players all over New York and the rest of the country instantly adopted it as part of their game.

What Magic Johnson and Michael Jordan did was combine all of the skills their pioneering predecessors—such as Luisetti and Monroe—introduced to the game and thereby make the multidimensional, athletic player the model for modern basketball. LeBron James, Kobe Bryant, Dwyane Wade, and many others demonstrate that fact every time they take the court.

New Prototypes

Today, we see taller players and better athletes. Exercise physiologists, strength and conditioning specialists, and "performance training" specialists are everywhere. Their expertise has helped players develop into athletes who are faster, stronger, more powerful, and more agile. Also, because of year-round training programs and off-season competition opportunities, players are constantly building their bodies and expanding their games beyond the defined role that they might have with their particular team. As a result of this, the days of assigning players strict perimeter or post designations are long gone.

Today, coaches seek players with athleticism and skills that transcend traditional positions. And even if this wasn't what coaches were looking for, it's the trend among the talent pool. Attempts to label this hybridization of roles with names such as *point-forward* and *forward-center* fail to add much insight to the exact role and function a player is asked to fulfill.

The reality of modern basketball is that all players—regardless of position—must be able to perform effectively in a variety of areas on both ends of the court. That's especially true for high school and college players who aspire to play at the next level. Coaches are looking for players of all sizes who can handle the basketball, make the outside shot, pass the basketball, take it to the hole, and play defense inside and out.

In short, player positions are much more loosely defined in modern basketball, and as a result, every athlete on the court must be prepared to play in the post area. So let's look at how this actually plays out at the highest levels using examples of athletes who have helped define these positional prototypes.

Centers on the Move

In the early 1980s, the basketball world was abuzz about a Nigerian-born post player at the University of Houston. Hakeem Olajuwon was very different from the centers who preceded him. At 7 feet tall (213 centimeters), he could outrun guards on the fast break, cover the court from baseline to baseline and sideline to sideline, claim seemingly every rebound, and cause matchup problems for any opponent nearly tall enough to guard him. Some people would say that Hakeem's emergence on the scene only fanned the flames of the abandon-the-post firestorm sweeping basketball. But what it really did was demonstrate that a player who could be called a "center" had a place in the modern game if that player could play the whole court.

Dwight Howard, Amare Stoudemire, and Emeka Okafor are a few current manifestations of the mobile big man who is going to score close to the basket, block shots, and run the court well. Such players can face up and shoot or drive, but they're most adept at back-to-the-basket maneuvers and power moves.

Traditional Posts

The very tall and strong center whose game effectively resides within 12 feet (3.7 meters) of the basket can still be a major asset. Players such as Shaquille O'Neal, Yao Ming, and Zydrunas Ilgauskas contribute to their clubs by being a big presence. These types of players require the opposing defense to sag and help a teammate trying to guard them on the low block. They also give opposing offensive players something to think about before trying to drive the lane.

The traditional post player must develop excellent footwork, good passing skills, solid screening technique, and a good touch around the hoop. As their primary scoring weapons, these players use turnaround bank shots and hook shots from close range, as well as put-backs and dunks. Young and developing tall players whose coordination hasn't caught up to their latest growth spurt must avoid becoming frustrated with temporary lags in progress. They also shouldn't be humiliated if someone refers to them as a "stiff." If they keep working at it and develop some signature skills, they'll have the last laugh.

The Long Outside-Insider

Another category for players who in the past would have been called "centers" is today's taller manifestation of a player such as Dan Issel. This prototype passes the ball well, sets good screens, and can drive to the hoop; however, this type of player is especially noted for being able to face up—in some cases from some distance—and knock down the shot.

When Tim Duncan joined the San Antonio Spurs as the first pick in the 1997 NBA draft, everyone wondered how he would mesh with the team's established star center David Robinson. Duncan proved it to be no problem as he demonstrated a wide range of skills, including a very accurate 18-foot (5.5-meter) bank shot. Labeled "The Big Fundamental," Duncan is still very difficult to guard because he can take an opponent outside and inside. His footwork is so good that he will fake an opponent out of his socks and end up with a layup.

In the past, it was rare to have a center or power forward who possessed such an array of skills. Now, big men who cannot shoot the outside shot (such as Ben Wallace) are a liability on the offensive end because their defenders drop off to help inside. Post players today need to be like Tim Duncan, who can hit the outside shot, cut to the basket, dribble, and pass the ball.

German-born Dirk Nowitzki of the Dallas Mavericks further extended the range of this prototype player with his tremendous shooting eye and perimeter moves. His outside skills are complemented by his improved driving ability and back-to-the-basket moves. Nowitzki is a matchup nightmare for everyone.

Duncan and Nowitzki (and more recently, Pau Gasol and Candace Parker) have shown that limiting a big and tall player to the low post makes no sense in today's game. These individuals are proof that excellent skills outside the lane area can be of great benefit in giving opponents even more problems in the paint. And, when called on to do so, their ability to perform those functions formerly performed by "centers" has been crucial to their team's success.

A deadly three-point shooter, seven-foot Dirk Nowitzki also has the ability to penetrate to the basket.

Double-Double Bigs

Another versatile big man role that prevails in today's game is filled by players who don't handle the ball or shoot from long range as effectively. Despite those limitations, these players are very active and usually wind up with double-digit points and rebounds at the end of the game. Jermaine O'Neal, Kevin Garnett, Marcus Camby, and Chris Bosh are examples. Though such players have strong mid-range games, the inside game is crucial to their success. Therefore, they must master the footwork, positioning, movement, and shot-blocking techniques in and around the lane to excel on both ends of the court.

The Big Athlete

Remember the days when a 6-foot, 5-inch (196-centimeter) player who had a strong inside game could excel at the professional level, even if the player didn't dribble or shoot the ball from the perimeter well enough?

Adrian Dantley and Charles Barkley are two such players who had great success. These players possessed great savvy around the hoop and had a real nose for the ball.

Teams today are reluctant to draft players who fit the old "small forward" label if those players lack an outside game to complement their strong interior game. This type of forward has been replaced by the big athletic player who can pop outside and take a shot in addition to being a constant threat to drive to the hoop. These players—including Vince Carter, Ron Artest, Carmelo Anthony, and Shawn Marion—often make the television highlights with their spectacular dunks. However, they actually have an array of offensive skills, and they apply many of them in the lane area. Ballhandling isn't a strength because these players are finishers more often than creators on the offensive end.

Specials

Kobe Bryant, LeBron James, and Dwyane Wade represent the cream of the crop in terms of athleticism, savvy on the court, and diversity and level of skill. These players follow in the tradition of Michael and Magic. They can handle and create on the perimeter, hit the outside jumper, or take the ball to the hoop for a scintillating dunk or gravity-defying alley-oop. They can also hold their own in the lane area, using turn-around jumpers, quick spin moves, and a variety of fakes that almost always result in a score or defensive foul. They can also guard bigger players in the paint on the defensive end because of their great vertical leaping ability.

In today's game, players who are 6-foot-4 (193 centimeters) and taller must become more versatile in order to gain more playing time and more success. Since most high school programs, male and female, use some type of motion offense—where players are free to cut, dribble penetrate, pass, and screen—the offensive effectiveness of all players is directly related to how many things they can do with the basketball. Developing an inside game that complements adequate outside skills is fundamental to their future achievements.

Young players who aspire to greatness must be aware that they need to develop guardlike skills, not only offensively, but defensively as well. During the off-season, tall players in high school or college should work on their ballhandling, outside shooting, dribbling, and defensive skills. By developing those skills, a player may become a "special" player or may develop into a player who fits one of the other prototypes prevailing in today's game.

The Big Man Camp and Tall Women's Camp were started for this very reason. Players who can transcend positions will be better players and will get to play. I could see the game evolving decades ago, and I made it a personal objective to develop the big player—both forwards and centers. Those who learned became very good players.

One method for doing this is to include the tall players in guard drills. Don't limit forwards and centers to the inside game. Make them handle the basketball in dribbling drills. Make them compete with guards in three-point shooting. Make them try those difficult passes. And make them play defense against quicker players on the perimeter. If tall players don't develop these skills, the game may leave them behind.

Smaller players who are destined to play more on the perimeter can also benefit from skills around the basket. That does not mean the smaller players should power the ball inside with jump hooks, drop steps, and up-and-under moves. Like the tall player, they should identify the talents they have and should use them to their advantage close to the basket. For example, quick players can develop very effective fakes that create space for open jump shots and clear drives to the basket; taller guards and forwards can increase their vertical jumps to get their turnaround jump shots off quickly and high in the air; stronger players can learn to use their backsides and legs to power inside for layups and short shots.

Some young basketball players already have good footwork on the perimeter when executing one-on-one moves. Why not take that footwork into the post and explore various ways to use it to an advantage? That philosophy is exactly what the Big Man Camps and Tall Women's Camps are all about. Players who take their already developed outside skills inside will be better able to develop an effective inside-outside game (better than the taller player who up to that point may have only experienced basketball close to the basket). It's more difficult for the inside player to learn the perimeter than it is for the perimeter player to expand his game into the post.

Conclusion

In today's game, the more you can do, the more you play. As more and more multidimensional players are emerging, the playing time for the players who can only shoot from the outside is in jeopardy. Although too early to tell, it seems that this type of player will become extinct in basketball. Only 12 spots are available on a basketball team. The ballhandling skill of today's taller players is beginning to rival that of the guards. Smaller players are becoming stronger and can jump higher than ever before. Older players and coaches have often been accused of "letting the game pass them by." It seems odd to be addressing the same warning to the young players, but it's true.

CHAPTER 13

Rebounding

It has been said, "The team that controls the boards controls the game." Is that an overstatement? If not, how does rebounding help determine the outcome of a game?

Without a doubt, the statistic that determines the "big picture" of a basketball game is points scored per possession. One point per possession will usually win a basketball game. A *possession* begins when one team gains control of the ball and ends when the other team gains control. For example, if team A shoots, gets the offensive rebound, and resets the offense, it is still the same possession. Only when the other team gains control—through a defensive rebound, turnover, or score—does the possession end. This definition results in both teams having almost the same number of possessions for a game. Therefore, the team with the highest points per possession will win the game.

That makes the factors that affect points per possession ever important. Those factors are shooting percentage, free throw percentage, offensive rebounds, and turnovers. On a bad shooting night, free throw percentage, offensive rebounds, and minimizing turnovers become even more important; success in these areas can make up for the lack of points scored from the half-court offense. It is not difficult to see how rebounding, both offensive and defensive, can influence the outcome of a game. Offensive rebounds can make up for turnovers and poor shooting. Defensive rebounds can keep the opponent's points per possession to a minimum. In other words, the team that controls the boards can control the game.

Coaches may be convinced that rebounding is a high priority that should be emphasized in practice. But what about those players who don't see the value and are unmotivated to be aggressive on the boards? What can be done?

Motivating Post Players to Rebound

Even as a young coach for the Los Angeles Lakers, Pat Riley understood the direct relation of rebounding to winning. Desperate to increase the rebounding efficiency of his inside players, he devised a statistical method of tracking individual rebounding performance. This system was not limited to simply tracking the number of rebounds a player obtained in a game nor the number of rebounds per minute played. Instead, Riley's system was designed to reveal two unconventional rebounding statistics: rebounding effort and rebounding efficiency. Here's how the system worked.

For all 82 regular season games, a separate statistician was responsible for keeping rebounding statistics on each of the Lakers' inside players. For example, one statistician was assigned to keep those statistics on Kurt Rambis. Table 13.1 shows the data recorded for Rambis for one game. The left column reveals that while Kurt was in the game, there were 20 rebounds that were possible for him to get. If a missed shot bounced completely to the other side of the basket from Kurt, no mark was entered. The 18 marked in the next column shows that out of the 20 possible rebounds, Kurt made 18 legitimate efforts. In other words, he made little or no effort only 2 out of 20 times. The fourth column lists the actual rebounds Kurt got—the same number found on the post-game stat sheet that evening. Statisticians were also assigned for Kareem Abdul-Jabbar, Bob McAdoo, Mitch Kupchak, and Swen Nater. The next day, the players were given their individual results that revealed some pretty hard facts.

The percentage in the third column represents the ratio of legitimate attempts (second column) to possible rebounds (first column), thereby revealing rebounding effort. The percentage in the fifth column compares rebounding attempts (second column) with actual rebounds obtained (fourth column), showing rebound efficiency.

As mentioned, Riley's system was not designed to show conventional rebound statistics. He had a hidden agenda in mind. Ultimately, he wanted to see an increased number of rebounds per minute from all participating players. But, instead of having the players focus on the number of rebounds per minute or game, he turned their attention to the percentage found in the third column of the chart—rebounding

Table 13.1 Kurt Rambis Rebound Chart

Possible rebounds	Rebound attempts	Percentage (rebounding effort)	Rebounds obtained	Percentage (rebounding efficiency)
20	18	90%	9	50%

effort. He set the bar at 90 percent and expected regular improvement from all players until the goal was reached.

The method to Riley's madness was this: He knew that if he could convince the players to focus on improving their rebounding effort, the number of rebounds per minute played would take care of itself. In other words, focusing on the process rather than the product would eventually yield the product.

Riley's bar of 90 percent was the goal. The day after each game, Riley met with each player to analyze the personalized chart and provide feedback. All players worked hard to improve each game, and regular improvement was expected. As effort percentage increased, efficiency percentage also increased. The result was that the players legitimately went for the rebound more and more as the season progressed, which increased the players' chances of getting possession.

The use of Pat Riley's chart also resulted in an additional by-product. Now in a race to see who was at the highest effort percentage, all five players became extremely competitive during practice sessions, especially the three nonsuperstars. These three players (Kupchak, Rambis, and Nater) kept a verbal tally of total rebounds obtained during scrimmages, and the player with the lowest tally treated the other two to dinner on the next road trip. For those three players, rebounding became a "game within a game." Riley's mission was complete.

As a master and student of sport psychology, Coach Riley understood that for motivation to last, it must be generated from within the player. Although he established the goal, he also allowed the individual statistics to help the players see where they stood in relation to the goal and produce the effort to improve. When self-improvement was noticed, nothing more needed to be said or done. Improvement was the motivator. In fact, when a player reached 90 percent effort, Riley didn't even acknowledge it. Had he done so, the player may have become satisfied because Riley was satisfied. The players became so engrossed in moving up in percentage that they bought into what Riley was after—the pursuit of perfection.

Highly motivated and skilled athletes such as Rambis, Kupchak, and Nater are conditioned to improvement; they will often work hours for one-half a notch up the improvement ladder. For this reason, they often don't require regular feedback on their status because they can recognize it themselves and don't need external impetus. In other words, they don't need to be stroked. This is not true for the younger, developing post players. At the lower levels of basketball, coaches are generally more hands-on, assisting the players' performances. This often involves providing constant feedback on how the subject is performing in relation to the objective, as well as providing information on how the player can improve. Developing players will encounter a lot of negativity. Therefore, for the younger player, we recommend another approach in addition to Pat Riley's statistical system—recognition of almost every bit of improvement.

We want to make it clear that the feedback we present to players at the camps is not praise in the normal sense of the word. Praise often implies a declaration that the observer is pleased. That would be providing extrinsic motivation. A coach can let players know that improvement has been noticed without implying that the coach is proud of them. For example, the coach can use statements such as "That is exactly the way it should be done," "Much better," or "That was the longest step you have taken so far." Instead of saying, "I'm so proud of you," the coach can say, "You should be proud of yourself" or "Look how you're improving." Such statements work wonders for young players and send the credit back where it belongs.

At the Big Man Camp, we get players who are already highly skilled and motivated. Most are stars at their respective levels. However, the footwork and defensive reading that we ask them to do are new to all of them; therefore, in a real sense, they are all beginners and will make many errors. The players at the camps are aware that we have taught footwork and defensive reading to many of the greatest players in the game, so it's natural for them to look for our approval. We do everything we can to avoid compensating players in this way. All they receive from us is information and an occasional smile, signifying that I recognize they are improving. It's amazing what a smile can do. I usually see increased effort, concentration, and self-esteem.

Individual Defensive Rebounding

Players must be taught the proper technique for defensive rebounding. When playing man-to-man defense, each player must realize the importance of screening the immediate opponent from the rebounding ball. We teach players to assume a low stance with the arms spread up and away from the body as soon as the shot is taken.

If the defensive rebounder loses contact with the opponent because of premature advancement toward the basket, many problems will be encountered. For that reason, immediate contact must be made (see figure 13.1a). The defensive rebounder must be proactive. If there is space between the screener and the offensive rebounder, the latter is able to go toward the basket with momentum that can help the height of the jump and increase timing. An immediate screen will deter the offensive rebounder from making an uninterrupted move to the ball. It also creates space for the defensive rebounder to make the move toward the rebound at the right time.

Space allows the defensive rebounder to jump at a 45-degree angle to the ball (see figure 13.1b). This angle enables the rebounder to protect

Figure 13.1 The defensive rebounder *(a)* initiates contact and then *(b)* must go get the ball.

the ball when returning to the floor after gaining possession. If the release from contact is made too soon, or the rebounder goes to the ball without blocking out, the jump will often be vertical, making it difficult to bring the ball down to the chin for protection. When this occurs, opponents who are close by will be able to jar the ball loose. In other words, the ball will be exposed. However, if the angle is 45 degrees, the ball is protected. In addition, this position often induces a rebounding foul by the opposing rebounder for reaching over and making illegal contact.

Because of their height advantage and proximity to the rim, exceptionally tall players do not need to hold the block out quite as long as shorter players because their height has already created space between their opponent and the ball. However, the player who is significantly shorter than the player to be blocked out must make the aggressive initial contact, hold the opponent away from the rim to create space, and move to the rebound at a 45-degree angle. Make no mistake—we are not talking only about centers and inside players; every player must practice blocking out as described, no matter where they are on the floor in relation to the hoop. The greater the mismatch in height, the sooner contact is made and the longer it is held.

One of the shortest centers to play professional basketball was Wes Unseld at 6 feet, 7 inches (almost 2 meters). A rookie in the 1968 to 1969 season with the Baltimore Bullets, Wes found himself on the shorter end of the height stick every night. To neutralize his opponent and play big, Wes became extremely skilled in making initial contact and maintaining inside position, all the while moving to the rebound. For those who were matched up against him, the word around the league was "Your legs will hurt after the game." Wes Unseld's method of making contact was to thrust his backside into the thighs of the opponents, often freezing them because of the impact. Opponents often backed away from him to avoid the collision, leaving them in horrible position for the rebound. If there is any doubt about whether a player can concentrate on blocking out and still come up with the ball, Wes Unseld puts that to bed. During his career, Unseld averaged 14 rebounds per game. Not only was Wes named Rookie of the Year, he was also the league's MVP during the same year. As a Washington Bullet, he won the NBA crown in the 1977 to 1978 season.

Quick enough to block shots, Wes Unseld was also strong enough to make hard contact and get to the rebound.

But no player in NBA history illustrated the perfect blocking out technique and 45-degree trajectory better than the Boston Celtics' Dave Cowens. At 6 feet, 9 inches (206 centimeters), Cowens competed against much taller players such as Wilt Chamberlain, Kareem Abdul-Jabbar, and Bob Lanier, who were skilled offensive rebounders. His height disadvantage forced him to practice a defensive rebounding method that was identical to Unseld's; he blocked out quick and hard and jumped like a jet to the rebound. But his rebounding technique had one additional characteristic: When obtaining possession of the ball in midair, Dave flared his legs as an eagle spreads its wings (as shown in the photo). This discouraged offensive rebounders from coming near and prevented immediate pressure.

NBAE/Getty Images

Though a small NBA center, Dave Cowens was an above-average rebounder.

Individual Offensive Rebounding

Some coaches hold rebounding in such high esteem that they make it a major part of each practice session. As discussed earlier, an offensive rebound is like a turnover for the other team. Being a good offensive rebounder takes initiative, resourcefulness, aggressiveness, and the relentless desire to come up with the ball. Contrary to what many may think, some of the greatest rebounders at both ends of the court seldom dunked the basketball. This shows that these players were workhorses and cared little about flare and flashiness. It may also imply that they were not the tallest players on the floor, and that was often the case. Effective rebounding has more to do with zeal than size. It has been estimated that 75 percent of all rebounds are recovered below the rim.

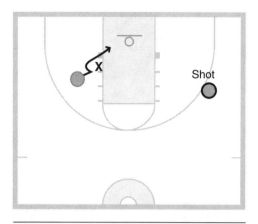

Figure 13.2 The offensive rebounder fakes away and then cuts to the desired position.

Offensively, the rebounder should initiate motion at the moment the shot is taken—or preferably, before the shot is taken. Great offensive rebounders are cunning and deceptive. First, they are extremely accurate in assessing what direction the ball will take after it hits the rim. Second, they make the initial move away from that direction, tricking the defensive rebounder into thinking they are going that way and opening up the area where they eventually want to end up (see figure 13.2). This is called *deployment of rebounding*.

Before Moses Malone and Dennis Rodman entered the NBA, many considered Paul Silas to be the best offensive rebounder in history. We consider him to be the most resourceful rebounder. Not only was Silas skilled at using fakes to get the position he wanted, but when he was unsuccessful, he was known to go out of bounds and then come back in to take the inside position. This certifies that he was a rebounder with the passion to get to the ball any way he could.

When Dennis Rodman entered the NBA in 1986, fans witnessed a dimension of offensive rebounding they had never seen before: incredible footwork and an unequaled pursuit of the basketball. On the defensive end of the floor, he was primarily concerned with stopping his assignment, who was often the most dangerous offensive player. Rodman was named the NBA defensive player of the year twice. On the offensive end, his focus was on helping his team regain possession of the ball if the shot was missed.

Rodman possessed great anticipation. Most offensive rebounders begin thinking about the rebound when the shot is taken or perhaps just before. Not so for Rodman. He was ever mindful of the ball and his position in relation to the man who was guarding him; therefore, he was ready to make his move when he had the greatest advantage. Often that move was initiated well before the shot was taken.

Some offensive rebounders can be stopped with the quick block out and hold, but players who were matched up against Dennis Rodman knew that the defensive rebound was never secured until it was secured. Dennis possessed another trait unique to him; in addition to being able to jump in all directions—as all great offensive rebounders can—the square footage he could cover was unequaled. Any opponent who casually went for what seemed like a sure rebound often found Dennis Rodman flying by him and stealing the rebound. Dennis was known to go so far as to fly horizontally to get the rebound, if need be.

Rodman was NBA rebounding champ seven years in a row and helped his teams win five NBA championships. Because of Rodman's antics, ejections, and need for attention, some people may argue that he was an individual who cared little about the team. But who can argue with five NBA championships? Dennis Rodman was a competitor who understood the value of offensive rebounding to team success, and he did his job better than anyone in history. Like him or not, he was a winner.

What can be learned from great rebounders such as Unseld, Cowens, Rodman, and Ben Wallace? Is it that athleticism is the key to rebounding effectiveness? Hardly! We could provide a list of players who were very good rebounders but were not extremely athletic. These players had great footwork and relentlessly pursued the missed shot.

Pat Riley's method of tracking effort can do much in the area of developing pursuit in players and bringing out their aggressiveness. Footwork also must be taught.

Rebounding Footwork

Body balance, footwork, and maneuvering speed were discussed earlier in the book as prerequisite movement skills for post play. Footwork includes pivoting and spinning. Developing maneuvering speed requires activities that involve changing direction and pace. The combination of the three prerequisite movement skills provides a good foundation for rebounding footwork. To be an effective rebounder, the player must be able to move and jump in that order. Any weakness in body balance, footwork, or maneuvering speed will cause a glitch somewhere in the total movement to the rebound. Defensive and offensive rebounding require different types of footwork.

Footwork for Defensive Rebounding

As previously mentioned, to move to a defensive rebound at the recommended 45-degree angle, the screener must initiate the contact and make the immediate block out before the offensive player begins to make the move to the rim. Making contact with the arm to the chest will stop some opponents, but the good ones need a quick backside to the thighs. Also note that the quick hit will eliminate the effectiveness of faking one direction to go the other, which is a key tactic for offensive rebounding (as previously described).

Spin Pivot

Initiating contact must be done quickly and assertively; there is no room for hesitation because the offensive rebounder must be stopped before beginning the move toward the rim. The moment the shooter begins the shooting motion, the screener makes a 180-degree spin pivot toward the offensive player and lands the backside into the thighs (see figure 13.3, *a* and *b*).

When the basketball is about to hit the rim, the defensive rebounder makes the move to the rim (see figure 13.3*c*). Holding position and waiting for the ball to almost reach the rim allows the defensive rebounder to read the direction of the possible miss. This decreases the chances of jumping in the wrong direction.

Figure 13.3 The defensive rebounder *(a)* makes a quick spin pivot for the block out; *(b)* has full contact, keeping the offensive rebounder away from basket; and *(c)* releases and moves to the rebound.

Front Pivot

Being proactive and making the first hit is ideal. However, there will be times when the offensive player makes a quick anticipatory move and the screener must react. When making the move to the rebound, the offensive player is limited to going to the middle or baseline. Therefore, the screener must learn two methods of footwork. If the opponent moves to the middle, the screener's baseline foot crosses over, and the front pivot is made (see figure 13.4*a*). The backside makes the impact on the opponent's thigh (see figure 13.4*b*). Also notice the position of the hands and the erect posture of the screener. The hands are up and ready for the rebound. The body is in balance, ready to move toward the basket at the correct time. Not only is the backside in contact with the opponent, the screener's entire back is also derailing any ploy to get by, such as a swim move.

Figure 13.4 The defensive rebounder *(a)* uses a front pivot to block out the defender going to the middle and *(b)* then blocks out the opponent and takes up space.

Reverse Pivot

If the offensive player makes a move toward the baseline, the screener makes a back, or reverse, pivot (see figure 13.5). Again, quick impact is made with the backside, but the back is also making contact.

A traditional method of blocking out involves using a reverse pivot no matter which direction the offensive player goes. However, because

Figure 13.5 The defensive rebounder uses a reverse pivot to block out the opponent going to the baseline.

obtaining and maintaining vision on the ball after it is shot is crucial to knowing when to release the block out and go to the rim, we recommend the front pivot when the offensive player makes the move to the middle. Besides making it possible to maintain ball vision from shot to rebound, this makes the player less likely to be faked in one direction.

Footwork for Offensive Rebounding

With the exception of the amount of contact with the arms and hands, the footwork for offensive rebounding can be compared to that of a defensive end in football who is attempting to get around the block and to the quarterback. It requires faking and an explosive change of direction. It also requires a countermove in case the first move is hindered.

Plan A—Faking and Exploding

Whatever part of the floor the offensive rebounder has determined the ball will bounce to, the player makes a fake in the opposite direction (see figure 13.6a). When the screener reacts, the offensive player changes direction by shooting the outside hand past the defender's chin toward the desired area and moving the outside foot over the defender's legs toward that same area (see figure 13.6b). When changing direction, the player accelerates toward the desired spot.

Figure 13.6 *(a)* The offensive rebounder fakes a baseline cut. *(b)* Shooting the arm past the defender's chin and stepping over the leg are key to gaining offensive rebounding position.

Plan B—Spinning

If the screener blocks the path to the desired area when the offensive rebounder is changing direction, the offensive rebounder must not stop and accept defeat; to counter the opponent's move, the offensive player makes a spin in the opposite direction. Position A was taken away, so the counter is to take position B (see figure 13.7). To spin quickly, the player's body must be low and in a vertical position, and the arms must not move too far out horizontally from the body, much like an ice-skater who is increasing the speed of a spin. However, the basketball player is not spinning in one spot; the spin is made simultaneously with motion toward position B.

Figure 13.7 Never get caught behind a block out. Here, the player is blocked out but is spinning to improve offensive rebounding position.

Team Rebounding—
The Forgotten 2-1-2 Triangle

Through the years, a number of coaches have written to me requesting information on the triangle of offensive rebounding. Why? The reason is very clear; these coaches realized that their teams were giving up fast break baskets at the expense of their half-court offense. Specifically, the coaches told me that when their teams turned the ball over or even missed a shot, their defense was not set. To protect against successful transition by the other teams, these coaches believed that a "prevent defense" (a system used to protect the lead) was necessary. In this way, they could send two or three players back when the shot was taken. However, this type of system seemed to slow the tempo they liked, released pressure on the opponent's ball handler, and was generally "passive" or "soft." I was able to assist these coaches by helping them understand that protection and aggression can, and should, both be part of the same system. Let me explain as I explained to them.

Floor balance is the key. If an offense doesn't have floor balance when a shot is taken, protection against transition is only a hope. A team has floor balance when there are no more than three players on the strong side, one player is at the top of the key, and one player is on the weak side. That's the beginning. When the shot is taken, three players take inside offensive rebounding responsibility, one player comes to the free throw line area to make an attempt at the long rebound, and the last player, the protector, is running back toward the half-court line (see figure 13.8).

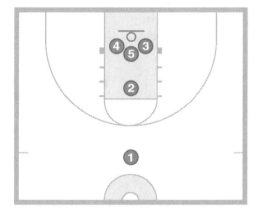

Figure 13.8   Ideal team offensive rebounding position: three inside rebounders, one long rebounder, and a protector.

Now here is how aggression and protection can coexist. Although the team is in a proactive alignment for the offensive rebound (the players are in position to get the rebound), it is also set to protect against transition. When the ball is retrieved by the other team, the three inside rebounders sprint toward the other end of the court. Not only are they able to get back on defense, more important, they are set to put pressure on the basketball, retard the advancement of the basketball, and press if they want to. Either the long rebounder or the protector advances toward the ball handler, and the other four players zone the rest of the court.

In a sense, the team is aligned much like a football defense that is protecting the lead with two minutes to go; it allows short passes and runs but nothing more than five or six yards (4.6 or 5.5 meters). However, the difference between that type of football defense and the one we are describing for basketball transition is *pressure on the ball*. Lead protection or "prevent defense" in football never includes the blitz; the quarterback usually has all the time he needs. In basketball, immediate pressure on the ball is applied, preventing the quick dribble through the defense. More important, in cooperation with the long rebounder and the others who are now zoning full court, the pressure on the ball eliminates the possibility of the long pass. So you see, aggressive offensive rebounding and effective transition defense is possible. Success is contingent on floor balance when the shot is taken.

When I listened to those coaches more closely, it became clear that the problem for most of them was their half-court offensive systems. Almost all of them ran some form of motion offense or passing game that lacked the structure necessary to have floor balance when a shot was taken. I told them that if they didn't make changes to address this issue, developing consistent defensive transition was going to be very difficult if not impossible.

In some cases, I drew diagrams of my "reverse action" offense, a derivative of the half-court offensive system used by the great Jimmy R. Needles, whose credentials rival those of just about any basketball coach in history. Phil Woolpert and I had the privilege of studying under Coach Needles at Loyola Marymount University in Los Angeles. One thing Phil and I learned was the importance of constant pressure on the basketball, especially when transitioning from offense to defense. When formulating my own offense, I was not about to compromise that part of game strategy. As Coach Needles passed on his transition system to me, I passed it on to those coaches who were so kind to write me.

Big Ben

Ben Wallace pursues rebounds with great effort.

© Icon Sports Media

If there is one word to describe Ben Wallace as a rebounder, it would be relentless. If Ben were included in Pat Riley's calculations, he would be near 100 percent in the effort ratio. Except in occasional offensive free throw situations, Wallace goes hard to the ball every time it is shot.

Wallace demonstrates a great balance between competitiveness and composure. He is able to compete at a high physical level, using his 250-pound (113-kilogram) sculptured body to scratch and claw his way to inside position, yet he never allows anything to get personal. It's interesting to see the frustration in his opponents as they see him grab one offensive rebound after another.

The closer the game and the more important the possession, the better the rebounder Ben Wallace becomes. This is often apparent when Ben's team is protecting a lead. When the opposing defense is gambling to get the interception and is focused on getting the first defensive rebound, Wallace regularly comes up with the offensive rebound, passing the ball back out to a guard to reset the 24-second clock.

Those who play and coach basketball understand the mentality of a Ben Wallace, but few rise to that level of intensity and relentlessness. The reason for this may be that the cause of the motivation of players such as Wallace is so difficult to put on paper or into words. And, because that mentality is nearly impossible to attain, perhaps that is why so few of this breed have emerged through the years.

But so far, we have addressed only the mental qualities of Ben Wallace that make him a great rebounder. Good rebounders always have great footwork, and Ben is no exception. Getting to an offensive rebound requires faking and quick changes of direction. It requires spinning, stepping over defenders' legs, and pivoting to initiate aggressive contact, which leads us to the last point of this chapter.

The tallest player may not be the leading rebounder. In fact, at the highest level of competition, the NBA, the center rarely leads the league in rebounding. It's the athletic, aggressive, and competitive forward that has the ability to get to the ball more often. Therefore, it behooves a team to develop all players as rebounders. Each time the offense takes a shot, rebounders should use footwork to get inside position and to retrieve the ball no matter where it bounces. Each time a shot is taken by the other team, all five players should block out quickly and aggressively, and all should go to the ball. As someone once said, "I will depend on my teammates to be co-rebounders, but I will go to the board as if it all depends on me." That's playing big.

Drills for Rebounding

More drills have probably been created for rebounding than for any other part of the game of basketball. However, to create the habit of blocking out and maneuvering for the offensive rebound, few drills are actually needed. The key is repetition and enforcement. Drilling provides repetition of making the right moves and increasing aggressiveness. Enforcing rebounding effort is done by constant monitoring and by using tools such as the Pat Riley chart. Here are three of the best rebounding drills.

Mass Defensive Rebounding

Divide all players into pairs and spread them in the half-court area, not too far apart but not so close that collisions may occur among pairs. Matching up by size is not necessary because the practice of competing against taller or quicker players is part of the game. Play big against big but mix it up a little. On the coach's signal—"shot"—the defensive rebounder spin pivots into the offensive rebounder (who attempts to avoid contact) and maneuvers to keep the opponent from going around. The defensive rebounder then makes a move toward the imaginary rebound, jumping at a 45-degree angle, gains possession, comes down to the floor, and makes the imaginary outlet pass.

In the same way, have defensive rebounders react to offensive moves to get around them, using the front or back pivot to make aggressive contact. To start, all offensive players will make the move to their left so screeners can practice the appropriate pivot. After sufficient repetition, offensive players move in the other direction. Later, or on the following day, the offensive players are given the freedom to choose a direction.

Mass Offensive Rebounding

Position the players the same as in the previous drill. On the coach's signal—"shot"—the offensive players fake a predetermined direction, shoot the hand

and leg through as they change direction, and explode past the screener. Then, they jump to get the imaginary rebound and jump again to make the imaginary put-back shot. For both defensive and offensive mass rebounding drills, one player should do at least three repetitions before the players switch from offense to defense. This will supply the repetition needed to begin creating the correct habit.

Five-on-Five Blocking Out and Offensive Rebounding

This is a good activity for drilling in habit and moving toward gamelike conditions. Five players are on defense, and five on offense. On the signal, offensive players become active and move around the key and perimeter. Two coaches are positioned on the perimeter, one on the right and one on the left (see figure 13.9). The coaches pass the ball back and forth until one shoots. When the shot is taken, defenders quickly find the thighs of their opponents, hold, and go to the rebound; the offensive players make cunning moves to get inside position. Coaches should correct every error. All defensive players must hit and hold, and all offensive players must fake, cut, spin, or whatever it takes to get to the rim. No offensive player should give up and concede position. No defensive screener should be outmaneuvered.

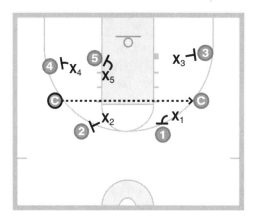

Figure 13.9 Five-on-five blocking out and offensive rebounding.

Conclusion

Much like half-court offense, productive team offensive rebounding is dependent on two factors: team alignment and individual plays. The spacing, player movement, and ball movement of an offensive pattern get the basketball into the hands of the best players, in their highest percentage areas. It is then up to the players to make the individual plays. Likewise, a team's offensive rebounding effectiveness increases when good spacing is created, as shown in figure 13.8 on page 166. It is then up to the players to make individual maneuvers to regain possession of the ball.

The obvious purpose of team alignment is to place players in position so that, wherever the ball bounces, one or more of them is in the vicinity to make an effort to get the ball. However, another purpose exists. Training the players to align each time a shot is attempted sends a message; offensive rebounding is part of winning basketball. Team alignment completes a facet of basketball that is directly related to winning, or, at least, maximizing a team's potential. What's left is to teach the players what Pat Riley was after: effort and a gut-burning desire to steal an extra shot at the hoop.

CHAPTER 14

Defense

My first meeting with Bill Russell, the great University of San Francisco Don and Boston Celtic, was when Bill played for USF. I had just taken over as head basketball coach at the University of California at Berkeley, and USF was on our schedule. At the time, I was aware that USF was one of the best teams in the West. But I didn't know that USF was so good that the team would win the next two national championships (1955 and 1956). They were also destined to set the record for consecutive wins in the NCAA by winning 60 straight games. What many people don't know is that during that streak, the Dons held opponents below 60 points 47 times. That USF team was one of the best—if not the best—defensive teams in NCAA history.

The coach at USF was Phil Woolpert, a former teammate of mine at Loyola University (and now a Hall of Fame inductee). Phil was a fine coach but not of the usual mold. He was extremely mild mannered and was considered a true "gentle" man—unusual for a Division I coach. Yet, most coaches of that era considered him a natural. As a high school coach, he had a respectable 63-29 record.

Phil put together a fine team. Little did I know that Bill Russell had become the top player on the West Coast. His ability to control a game via the blocked shot was the key to the success of the USF Dons. In my first game against USF, Russell blocked the first 12 shots my team took. During a break, my center told me, "Coach, I've tried every shot I know, and he's blocked every one of them." But Bill Russell was not the only great player on that team. K.C. Jones was a fantastic guard with high basketball intelligence, quick moves, great touch, and excellent defensive abilities. The rest of the team was made up of fine young players who knew how to play the team game. Yes, Russell had a good supporting

Bill Russell controlled games through his intimidating shot-blocking ability.

cast, but make no mistake—Bill Russell made that team into champions.

Playing against Bill Russell was a real problem, not only winning-wise, but also psychologically. The blocked shots stayed in the minds of my players for weeks. I made up my mind that if we were ever going to play against Russell again, I would compose a game plan that minimized his shot blocking. I scheduled USF the following year (1956), Russell's and Jones' senior year. I can tell you that the game and the preparation for that game was most enjoyable. USF had won 58 straight games; we were supposed to be number 59.

For me, one of the enjoyable things in coaching is being able to create a game plan when the odds are heavily against my team winning. My thought was to keep Russell busy on one side, reverse the ball, and run a quick two-man game on the other side before Russell could recover. To keep Russell on one side, the plan was to force him to come over and guard my center, who was a good outside shooter. I created a play (with options) that I thought would work.

At the beginning of the first practice preparing for the game against USF, the first thing I did was tell my players, "Russell is not going to block one shot this game." Their eyes sparkled when I said that. At one end of the court, I drew a line from the mid-court line, dividing the half court in two. I had a guard hold the ball at the point on the strong side, where one forward was stationed low and my center was at the wing. The other two players were positioned on the other side of the floor (see figure 14.1).

As mentioned, my center was a great shooter from 16 to 18 feet (about 5 meters). Therefore, since he was at the wing, Russell had to guard him tight. This would cause Russell to start as far away from the players on the other side as possible. But causing him to start there wasn't enough; I had to keep him there, because he was quick enough to sprint to the other side and block almost any shot. In other words, I had to keep him occupied guarding my center.

I showed the players how I wanted the low-post forward to set a back screen on Russell and how that screen would keep him occupied and sealed from the other side (see figure 14.2). The plan was to reverse the ball quickly and get a shot on the other side while Russell was attending to the screen placed on him. However, that back screen play for my center was a good play in itself. If Russell dropped to the basket to avoid the screen, my center received the ball for the jump shot. If Russell continued to play him tight, he cut off the screen to the basket for the reception and score.

My screening forward didn't let Bill drop below the screen. He made sure that the screen was set effectively. More important, he

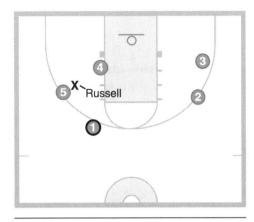

Figure 14.1 Initial position of the half-court offense against USF.

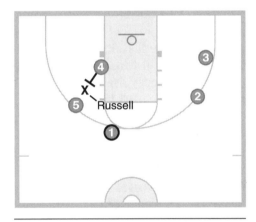

Figure 14.2 The low-post forward sets a back screen on Bill Russell, keeping him occupied on the left side.

made sure that he held the screen so that Bill wouldn't be able to get to the other side quickly when the ball was moved there for the two-on-two.

At the beginning of the game, the plan worked perfectly. We had a lead of 15-3 after 14 minutes of play. But USF had K.C. Jones, the best backcourt player I had seen.

Part of my strategy was to keep Jones from pressing my ball handler bringing the ball up the court. USF had the best full-court pressure in the country. So I told my players, especially K.C.'s assignment, "When USF takes a shot, sprint to the other basket." It worked. Jones, USF's best backcourt defender, went back with my guards, and I had my biggest forward bring the ball up the court. But K.C. wised up and started staying back to press. This made it more difficult to advance the ball, and we lost it a time or two. USF began to catch up.

To mix things up, I would have my players show zone press when we were actually in a man-to-man, and vice versa. This was designed to keep K.C. and the USF players somewhat off rhythm. However, the problem with this tactic was that Phil Woolpert had been my assistant, and he used the same tactics that I did (only more effectively because he had better players).

But I had another problem. My center fouled out soon after halftime. He had made 10 points, mostly on outside shots when Russell gambled to help on the other side. As a team, we only had 18 when it happened. That forced me to put in my "walk-on" 240-pound (109-kilogram) backup center. We had possession of the ball with 16 minutes remaining in the game and were up by a small margin. I ran out of players, and the six I had were really tired. USF grabbed the lead.

We passed the ball from guard to guard to my reserve center on the wing. However, Russell didn't consider him a threat and dropped below the basket to zone the court. My captain came over to me and asked, "What do we do?" I told him to stall because we needed energy to full-court press the last 5 minutes of the game. The USF fans wanted to kill me, but the Cal fans loved it. Russell stayed in the paint area and my center, repeatedly, had the ball on the wing. As he held the ball, it kept the game close and I was short on bench help.

However, as planned, with 5 minutes to go, we switched into a full-on, aggressive, full-court press that was successful in gaining a few extra possessions. But it proved to be too little, too late, as USF ended up winning the game 33-24. We came closer to beating that historical team than anyone else did in the two years they dominated college basketball. Because of that one game, for years after, my players believed in my game plans.

Cal wasn't the only team to spend an entire week preparing for USF and create new plays and strategies halfway through a season. Every team was out to beat the Dons, and almost every team lost trying. I can go on about how that game, though lost, benefited my players and me. But that's not the point in this chapter on defense. The point here is how a great defensive post player can change the entire game to the benefit of his team. As we will see in this chapter, a post player who is able to defend one on one, direct the team defense, and be a defensive stopper as the last line of defense can literally change the game. A Russell-type defensive force will affect the minds of every opposing player and change the offensive strategy of every opposing coach.

The remainder of this chapter is devoted to four areas that I feel very strongly about: one-on-one defense, communication, competitiveness, and defending the ball screen.

Three Dimensions of an Effective Post Defender

Not every center can block shots as Bill Russell did. In fact, many cannot block shots at all. Fortunately, there are other defensive components that make the complete post defender. To be complete, the post defender must be skilled in the following three areas: stopping an opponent one on one, being vocal as a team defensive director, and having a competitive spirit.

One-on-One Defense

When playing college basketball for UCLA, the great Bill Walton made it his personal goal to block the first shot his man took in a game. He said, "When I block that shot, I don't have to worry very much about that guy the rest of the game. All I have to do is fake, and he'll pass the ball instead of shoot. This enables me to put more concentration on helping my teammates" (personal conversation, about 1995). Bill was able to do that most of the time. However, the average center is not as talented.

But the point is not the block. The point is that Bill had to find a way to get to that shot when it was taken. Some players were limited offensively, and Bill had little difficulty getting to the shot. Against those players, he acted as if he was going to let them shoot. But when they did, he was right there to send that shot to a teammate, beginning a fast break. Against more talented players, he had to figure out how to get to the shot to block it.

Bill Walton's goal was not necessarily to block the shot. Rejections were a by-product of good post defense, which Walton achieved by concentrating on these principles: getting position, forcing the offensive player to his weakness, and putting pressure on every shot. Time and again, when a poor shot was taken and Bill's hand was there, the ball would find it.

Getting Position

The first step toward stopping a low-post player, one on one, is to get position before the ball is passed. The chance of a completed pass from wing to post is increased if the offensive post player is positioned in the ideal position—directly between the ball and the basket. Tex Winter calls this positioning "the line of deployment." If the offensive player is not in this position, the defender can assume that spot and be in good position to deny or steal the pass. If the forward has the ball on the perimeter but below the free throw line extended, the offensive post player is forced to move toward the baseline and toward the block.

For that reason, the defender should be alert to take the spot between the ball and the basket before the offensive player does.

Most offensive post players operate best when they are positioned in the mid-post area. Some, such as Shaquille O'Neal, like to start a move a little closer to the block (in Shaquille's case, this is because the range of his jump hook is limited to inside 6 feet [1.8 meters]). The post defender should try to make the offensive player receive the ball around the block area or even lower, instead of at the mid post. This will result in a lower-percentage shot because the baseline move is eliminated—there is no room for the player to make a baseline move.

Wherever the offensive post player positions—at the block, mid post, or even higher—the defender should assume a tight position on the high side (the defender should be closer to the half-court line than the offensive player is). This defensive positioning is recommended for the following reasons:

1. The angle of the pass from wing to post goes away from the base-line, higher in the air, so the pass has a chance of being picked off by a guard.

2. The defender can gain more favorable rebounding position when a shot is taken from the perimeter.

3. Playing the high side often causes the offensive post player to drop lower, down to the block, where the defender gains an advantage. The post defender is most vulnerable when the offensive player is at the mid post.

4. If the basketball is passed to the corner, the post defender can still deny the pass by rolling over the top and fronting. Weak-side defensive help should be available.

Forcing Offensive Players to Their Weakness

Wherever the offensive post player receives the basketball, the defender's next job is to force that player to the weakness. Every player has a weak-ness, even the greatest scorer in professional basketball history, Kareem Abdul-Jabbar. No one was able to prevent Kareem from shooting the sky hook on the right side of the floor. But when he was positioned on the left side, intelligent defenders took away the hook shot across the key and made Kareem turn to the baseline for the turnaround jump shot, his weakest move. Pat Riley, well aware of this, created plays to Jabbar's strength, passing to him in the middle of the lane and on the right side.

But most players are not that skilled and don't have coaches and teammates who can get them the ball so they can use their strengths exclusively. The wise defender studies that player, uncovers what the strength is and what the weakness is, and devises a plan to take away the strength and force the player to use the weakness. At the high school, college, and even the professional levels, most post players do not have a complete arsenal; they don't have counters that are polished.

A generally effective method for guarding the post player with the basketball is the following. The defender assumes a stance behind the offensive player and slightly to the baseline, taking away the baseline move; the defender's baseline-side forearm is gently into the offensive player's lower back, and the other arm is up to discourage the move across the key (see figure 14.3*a*). When the player begins to make the

Figure 14.3 *(a)* Excellent initial defensive position to prevent the baseline move and discourage the move across the key. The defender *(b)* cuts off the move across the key and *(c)* crowds the offensive player to prevent a baseline move and encourage a pass back out to the perimeter.

move into the key, the defender steps in the path, making the player move away from the hoop (see figure 14.3b). This will cause a poor shot attempt, stop the player, or cause a countermove toward the baseline. If that player turns to the baseline, the defender crowds the player by bellying up (see figure 14.3c). Most often, the dribble will be picked up and the ball passed back out to the perimeter.

Pressuring Every Shot

Blocking a path to the basket is not enough to define good post defense. The post defender must pressure the shot every time it is taken. Just to be clear, I am not talking about 99 percent of the time a shot is taken; I am talking about 100 percent. That offensive post player must sense the threat of the blocked shot each time a shot goes up. However, pressure on the shot must not come at the sacrifice of fouling the shooters.

This requires excellent footwork. Imagine an offensive player faking the hook shot across the key, stepping back for the jump shot, faking that jump shot, and stepping back across the key for the hook shot. For the defender to elevate when necessary (only after the offensive player has left the feet for the shot), that player must maintain a crouched position, have the hands about shoulder height, and be in balance with the back almost vertical (see figure 14.4). Any deviation from this position will cause the player to wind up to jump. In other words, if the legs are upright, the defender needs to bend down and then jump. That bend down is winding up, which takes time and destroys timing. If the player's hands are down, they must be raised before jumping—again winding up and taking time. The same is true for the vertical back. Having to bend the back down and then up to jump takes time.

Figure 14.4 A crouched position with hands at shoulder height and back straight is essential for quick elevation when attempting to block the shot.

The Defensive Director

The second dimension of a good defensive player is communication. Communication between teammates is unnecessary on offense because the movement of the basketball and players is determined by the defense. For example, when executing the screen-and-roll, the guard's decision to come off the screen or reverse back is determined by what the defensive guard does. There is no need for a teammate to say, "Cut back." The opposite is true for defense. Communication is extremely important for team defensive success. In fact, without communication between defenders, no team defense can come close to its potential.

All defenses have the same primary goal: to stop the penetration of the basketball. If a team can be forced to shoot a majority of their shots from the perimeter, the defensive team has a good chance of coming out on top. But most offensive plays are designed to penetrate the defense in order to create an inside score or an open outside shot (if the defense collapses). How can a defensive team limit the penetration? The answer is communication.

Because the post defender is usually closer to the baseline and more toward the center of the half court than the other defenders are, that player is often in the best position to communicate to the rest of the team. Therefore, at the heart of a good team defense is a post defender who directs the defense by communicating to her teammates.

The Duke University Blue Devils do as good a job of team defensive communication as any college team—and better than most NBA teams. It is a coordinated effort to stop ball penetration and sustain defensive pressure on the ball and passing lanes. The "center" of that communication is always the center. Because he can see everything, he is the director.

But communication alone is not sufficient. The communication must be intelligent and specific. Telling post players to simply "communicate" will not create clear communication. They must know what to say in each defensive situation. Like maneuvers, communication must be practiced to perfection. The following are the most important things that the post defender must communicate.

"High Post" or "Low Post"

When the offense first sets up, the post defender must inform teammates whether the offensive post player is positioned high or low. As the play is developing, any change in post position must be communicated. Keeping teammates informed of the location of the center is important because if the defensive post player is taken away from the basket toward the high post (see figure 14.5), the wing players must do all they can to prevent baseline dribble penetration (because there is no post help). In

Figure 14.5 The defensive post player is taken away from the basket toward the high post.

addition, the guards must know that if a pass is made to the wing, a high-post screen is a possibility. A simple call of "High post" is all that's necessary to put a specific team defensive adjustment into play.

If the offensive post player is positioned low, the post defender yells, "Low post." This informs wing defenders not to allow middle penetration. The post defender cannot help on middle penetration when the offensive post player is at the block, because a simple dish pass will result in a layup. However, the defensive post player is in position to provide some help on baseline penetration. Usually, a hedge and recover is enough to derail a dribbler.

"I've Got Help" or "Switch"

When dribble penetration occurs during a play, the post defender lets the teammate who got beat know that help is there to stop further penetration (see figure 14.6). "I've got help" communicates just that—there is assistance. If the post defender sees that the teammate is completely

Figure 14.6 The post player yells "Switch" and moves to cut off the loose driver.

beat and has no chance of recovering to help stop the offensive player, a call of "Switch" is in order. This is a signal for the teammate to drop and cover the offensive post player.

"Screen Right" or "Screen Left"

When the offensive post player is screening on the ball, the post defender yells either "Screen right" or "Screen left" (see figure 14.7). This must be done before the screen is set so the teammate has time to adjust.

For some players, communication is natural; for others, getting them to talk on defense is like getting them to be excited about getting teeth pulled. But that is beside the point. Post players *must* be verbal communicators. Because we are well aware that some players are natural communicators and some are not, we limit the things they are required to say, and we are very specific about what they must say. We believe a limited curriculum makes it easier to teach and learn.

Figure 14.7 The post defender alerts the teammate by calling "Screen left."

Competitive Spirit

The third dimension of a skilled post defender is a competitive spirit. Read the words of Grantland Rice, famed sportswriter during the Great Depression, as he presents the spirit of one who loves to tackle a difficult challenge.

The Great Competitor

Beyond the winning and the goal,
Beyond the glory and the fame,
He feels a flame within his soul,
Born of the spirit of the game.

And where the barriers may wait,
Built by the opposing gods,
He finds a thrill in bucking fate
And riding down the endless odds.

Where others wither in the fire,
Or fall below some raw mishap,
Where others lag behind and tire,
Or break beneath the handicap,
He finds a new and deeper thrill
To take him on the uphill spin,
Because the test is greater still
And something he can revel in.

John Wooden often quotes this poem when he speaks of a competitive spirit. I know of no other piece of literature, small or exhaustive, that captures this concept as well as Grantland Rice did in the previous poem.

The reason this poem is included in this chapter is because I want players and coaches to know that—well beyond the fundamentals and drills presented to develop a great post defender—the most important muscle used for defense is not in the legs, back, or arms. That muscle is in the chest area and is called "the heart."

Why are some players seemingly content with getting beat while others take it as a personal insult? Why do some players do nothing in between games to prevent repeated embarrassment while others work their tails off to try to fix whatever it was that caused the opponent to score so easily? Why do some have such a cavalier disposition when an opponent makes a score while others appear to burn with a competitive spirit that confidently dares the opponent to come back and try it again? Perhaps the answer lies so deep within human nature or is so buried in heredity that we will never know.

Those who are fortunate to be fiercely competitive, such as Bill Russell, can only talk about it but have difficulty teaching it. They can attempt to teach the "how" and inspire it, but the bridge between the word and the hearer's legitimate attempt to make the change is big—we rarely see a transformation of the timid to the tough. In other words, beyond the realm of teaching, it is the hunger to shut down an offensive player that causes the development of quick feet and jumping ability, not vice versa.

Sound discouraging? Before we relegate the destiny of greatness to something beyond what can be learned, we must point out that our experience has shown that it is not impossible for a player to change from noncompetitive to competitive. We have seen some players who were once acquiescent to a challenge but morphed into defensive beasts who want to "shut you down." If beaten, they will come back and "beat you." I have seen it; therefore, I know that within some young players there lies a competitor that is worth the effort of attempting to bring it out.

How do we do it? The best way is by using the drills described in this chapter and by presenting examples of athletes who had a passion for defense. Perhaps drilling will give a player a taste of the addictive power of controlling an offensive player and executing the blocked shot. Perhaps stories of great competitors of the past will find the pilot light.

Defending the Ball Screen

Because of the motion offense and especially the flex offense, the screen away from the ball has ruled the college and high school games for many years. But today, we are seeing more and more screening on the ball at all levels. The most difficult position for the post defender is when the offensive post player sets the screen on the ball.

Here's the dilemma: If the defensive center stays with his man, the cutter may very well come off the screen for an open jump shot or drive to the basket. If the defender hedges and helps too long, the screener will roll to the basket and receive the pass for the layup or short jump shot.

To derail the ball screen, we offer two possible methods as counters: switching and trapping. The key to deciding which to use is to evaluate the ball screen's complete effectiveness. "Complete" includes what the offensive players do after the screen is completed. For example, if they don't take advantage of mismatches well, the switch defense may be the best tactic. If they do, trapping the ball handler may be the best way to go. Of course, we are assuming that the ball screen is a dangerous weapon for the offensive team if the play is guarded without switching.

Switch Defense

In all screening situations, the screener is the most dangerous player. If the switch is loose and the screener can slip to the basket, even before the interchange, the screener may receive a pass and penetrate the defense. Therefore, the screener's defender *must* stay between the screener and the basket until the cutter's defender can assume that position. Before the interchange, both defenders play their offensive players tight.

Trapping Defense

When trapping the ball handler after that player has used the screen, the trap must be aggressive, and both defenders must keep their hands up, discouraging the pass to the middle. The only pass allowed is a lateral pass to the perimeter. When that pass is made, the ball handler's original defender stays on the player who passed the ball while the screener's defender rotates straight to the basket, looking for the open offensive player.

As soon as the trap is administered, the remaining three defenders zone the half court, playing the possible passing lanes for the steal but always being conscious to shut down any vertical pass into the lane area. When the ball is passed out of the trap, those players match up to strong-side offensive players and communicate to the rotating player where his new assignment is.

Drills for Defense

The following drills are designed to help the defensive player develop good habits in the following areas: timing, agility, vertical jumping, and knowing when to leave the feet when pressuring a shot.

When to Leave the Floor

The defensive player who can elevate and block the shot will be in the stat book. But the player who can elevate after the shooter leaves his feet and still contest the shot will be in the game. Jumping before the shooter jumps is assuming that no collision will occur. But there is no guarantee. Jumping after the shooter leaves her feet makes it possible for the defender to jump "with" the shooter, a concept Bill Walton is a strong advocate of.

This requires balance and the ability to jump in any direction quickly and with an adequate degree of elevation. The novice shot blocker will start from scratch when learning this skill. The more experienced defender who is in the habit of jumping prematurely will be replacing an old habit with a new one.

Figure 14.8 The defender *(a)* prepares to jump and *(b)* elevates vertically to contest the shot.

We begin with vertical elevation. The offensive player is in a crouched position and is holding the basketball, ready to shoot; the defender, about four feet away (a little more than one meter), is also crouched with the hands about shoulder height, ready to jump (see figure 14.8*a*). The shooter shoots, and the defender contests the shot (see figure 14.8*b*), leaving the floor after the shooter does. Lots of repetition will develop the habit of leaving the floor at the right time. For a more advanced version, the shooter may fake first and then shoot. From the defender, we are looking for good judgment and elevation.

Figure 14.9 *(a)* The defender moves with shooter to get to the ball. *(b)* The defender avoids contact by jumping back as the shooter is jumping forward.

Next, we proceed to horizontal and vertical jumping. The offensive player can shoot any of the following four shots: the fallaway jump shot, the power layup left, the power layup right, or the jump shot over the defender (see figure 14.9).

Goaltending

Goaltending in a game is a violation. Goaltending as practice produces timing and improves the vertical jump. Although this drill promotes goaltending as practice, there is no fear of the habit carrying over to the game.

With a player who can goaltend the shot, we begin by having the coach take one dribble and a hook shot in the key, about four to six feet from the basket (one to two meters), which provides enough space for the defender to get between the shooter and the basket. The post defender comes from the weak side, times the jump, and goaltends the shot (see figure 14.10). If the player cannot get above the rim, the coach shoots short, and the player goaltends the ball where he can.

Figure 14.10 The player goaltends a hook shot.

The player next goaltends short bank shots. The coach begins slightly outside of the block, and the player begins in a weak-side help position (see figure 14.11*a*). The coach takes one dribble, steps just inside the block, and delivers a shot that is directed at the top of the rectangle above the basket. The trajectory is determined by the jumping ability of the defender; the coach uses a trajectory that gives the player a chance at goaltending the shot after it makes contact with the backboard. When seeing the coach move toward the goal, the defender leaves the middle position, comes to a two-footed stop, and jumps to goaltend the shot (see figure 14.11*b*). After developing timing and the habit of going after every shot, the player can begin to work on contacting the ball at the top of its flight or as it is still going up.

Repeat as many times as needed, and practice the drill on both sides of the key. The defender's timing will improve, and that timing will increase the vertical height of the jump. As mentioned, when the coach feels comfortable that the player is ready, the coach instructs the player to attempt to make contact with the ball at the peak of its flight or before. In either case, a key teaching point—besides leaving the feet after the shooter—is that when attempting to

Figure 14.11 The defender *(a)* is on weak side, ready to provide help, and then *(b)* jumps high to goaltend the bank shot.

block the shot, the defender should keep the elbow above the head after the attempt. This will ensure that the player does not "swat" at the ball, bringing the arm down and possibly fouling the shooter. Although the stated object here is to actually make contact with the shot, the realistic goal is to get the hand between the ball and the basket, causing a distraction. The defender will be surprised to find that some players shoot the ball right into the defender's hand.

The repetition of attempting to block the shot develops a habit of going after the basketball every time it is shot. Once the habit is created, the player can be more selective about which shots to go after and which shots not to. Of Bill Russell, it was said, "All of us knew that Bill blocked about five shots per game. The problem was, when driving to the hole, I didn't know if my shot was going to be one of those five."

Bill Russell on Guarding Wilt Chamberlain and Kareem Abdul-Jabbar

Bill Russell sees the game of basketball as a combination of a vertical game and a horizontal game. The vertical game is played mostly under the basket when the ball is being shot and defended in close. The horizontal game is everything else before the shot, such as running up and down the court and moving around the half-court area.

Bill tried to make Wilt play the horizontal game as much as possible. Out of a 48-minute game, he tried to get Wilt to play 30 minutes of horizontal basketball—forcing Wilt to run up and down the floor trying to catch him when Bill was on offense, or making Wilt take the fallaway jump shot rather than the dunk (vertical).

On the defensive end, Bill began by getting to the low-post spot that Wilt wanted. Now Wilt had to move him out, which distracted Wilt from his usual routine. Wilt had a good turnaround jump shot, but he knew that Bill could block it in close. By going after Wilt's jumper, Russell made him fade away more than he was used to, lowering his percentage.

Russell never got the chance to guard Kareem Abdul-Jabbar; he retired just before Kareem's rookie year. However, in his book *Russell Rules*, he writes that he would play Kareem similar to Wilt. He states that because Kareem's vertical game was so good, the first thing he would do when playing against him would be to force him into a horizontal game of running up and down the court, causing him to expend more energy. Kareem liked to jog from block to block. That wouldn't happen against Russell or someone would have a layup on the other end.

Defense on Kareem would begin as soon as he crossed the half-court line. Russell would stand on the spot that Kareem wanted, making him begin his move one step farther away from the basket. Bill, being left-handed, would be in perfect position to put pressure on Kareem's right-handed hook shot. Defending the sky hook was all about footwork. When Kareem began his move, Bill would slide along his belly and get to the hook shot with the left hand. Also, Bill did not rule out the possibility that he would give Kareem a good dose of strategic conversation during the contest.

Conclusion

In a real sense, the game of basketball is a game of control. Each team is attempting to control the other in some way. Teams that up the pace of the game are attempting to cause the other team to play at a pace it is not used to. Teams that slow it down and play "ball control" are trying to do the same. The concept is "If I can control you and get you to do what I want, I have an advantage." This is not only true for basketball but for all sports—individual or team. For example, a tennis player who does not believe she can win a game of hitting from the baseline will come in to the net—in that way, the player takes away the opponent's strength. To counter, the opponent hits the ball deep, keeping the other player at the baseline.

Individual defense is no different. Bill Russell's defensive strategy on Wilt Chamberlain was to control Wilt by getting him to play a horizontal game—something to Bill's advantage. In other words, effective post defense is not reactionary; it's proactive. As Bill Russell and Bill Walton did, players are wise to study opponents, take away their strengths, and force them into situations that diminish the chances of a score.

CHAPTER 15

Instruction and Development

In a chapter about instruction and how it relates to a player's basketball development, it is tempting to provide a list of general teaching principles. However, that would do little to share the way I look at the purpose of the teacher and teaching. Therefore, I have included those topics that I believe are the most important for the basketball coach as a teacher. These topics include teaching players the "why," helping players with physical and mental issues that can affect shooting, teaching ambidexterity, using the whole-part method of teaching, and using a systematic approach to teaching post moves.

Teach the "Why"

One method of classroom teaching is lecture and testing. The professor spits out information, the students take notes, and the students are expected to regurgitate that information on an exam. A more effective and long-lasting method of teaching is based on a balance of didactic instruction and inquiry. Students are encouraged to inquire about the information they are presented, which results in more contextual relevancy for the instruction. In the context of teaching basketball, players who are taught to ask questions will discover the reasons why a particular way of doing things is best.

For example, a shooter in basketball normally needs space in order to get off a shot in rhythm and with a fluid motion. Ball fakes can help, but they are usually lateral fakes. To create the necessary space to allow the normal mechanics of releasing the shot, the best strategy for the shooter is to use foot fakes. Many foot skills can be added to a player's repertoire of shots, but players must be taught the fundamentals of each shot, the best situations for each shot, and the reason—the "why"—for using the shot. At the Big Man Camp, we teach counters for every way the defense can play. Each time a countermove is presented, the coaches teach the "why." For example, when a player initiates the reverse pivot after receiving the ball at the wing, the defense may react by retreating; in this situation, we teach players to immediately come back to a jump-shooting position. The "why" is that space has been created to get the shot off.

One of my most regular Big Man Camp participants was Purvis Short, a forward who was drafted in the first round by the Golden State Warriors. Purvis was one of the purest and most accurate shooters I have ever seen in the NBA. He had a shot that reached a height that few players achieved—a high-arching shot that was tremendously accurate.

In Purvis' rookie year, he started the NBA season with great success. He was given room to execute the shot. However, in the NBA, defenses make adjustments that often demand a change for the shooter. As the season progressed, Purvis experienced more and more pressure on that jump shot. His points diminished and so did his playing time. There had to be an answer for a player who had the shooting touch of Purvis.

The summer Big Man Camp helped Purvis equip himself with the counter. Each day, I would take Purvis to a side basket and have him work on a reverse drive to the basket after receiving the pass at the wing. I had him practice reverse driving from both sides of the court, using opposite hands. In that way, he developed the weaker hand—the left. We did this routine each day for about three days. Purvis had never driven the ball much in college. Open courts and on- and off-ball screens helped him get the open shot. None of these required footwork or foot skills to any extent.

After three days, I told Purvis I was going to have a player play him physically and tight on the ball. I also told him that I wanted him to strongly reverse drive to the basket as he had practiced. He was now comfortable with the reverse footwork, so he was able to beat the over-playing defender for easy baskets. I called a brief time-out and whispered to Purvis that I wanted him to take the reverse step but not to go forward; I told him to try coming back to a shooting position after the reverse step and see what happens. I had urged the defender each time to better defend Purvis' drive. I tossed the pass to Purvis, who gave a deep reverse step and then faced up to the basket. His defender was 6 feet (almost 2 meters) away from him, and Purvis drilled the open outside shot. Purvis had a big smile and said now he knew why I had spent so much time teaching him the reverse drive and step. Later, Purvis picked up a move that I have taught for almost 30 years—the Kiki move—a step back move that creates space when the defender is staying with an offensive player's drive. Kiki Vandeweghe perfected this maneuver. Both Purvis and Kiki were among the NBA scoring leaders for many years. One of the keys to their success was that they learned the "why."

Have Insight and Patience

When teaching the mechanics and fundamentals of shooting, all the mental and physical demands must be taken into consideration. Over my many years in the game, I have seen many great shooters, and I have come to the conclusion that successful shooting can be likened to successful batting in baseball. When I think of all the great hitters I have seen in person or on TV, I have always been struck by the differences in their stances at the plate. Joe DiMaggio had a real spread stance. Barry Bonds has a closed stance. Ted Williams' was not a closed stance but more spread. Willie Mays differed from all of them. Mel Ott raised his right foot. Al Simmons stepped in the bucket. The one thing all these players had in common was that the fat end of the bat, more often than not, was the hitting surface because they had confidence in their stances. If you analyze the great shooters of basketball, regardless of stance, you will note various common mechanics of release and follow-through. The important thing is not necessarily the position of the feet, but rather the consistency of the shooter's form as it relates to the release of the shot.

Some NBA players, such as Larry Bird, spent countless hours daily during the season to maintain their consistency of release and follow-through. A "soft ball" is often the result of a "soft touch." The shot dies on the ring, which leads to many baskets made. The soft touch seems to come naturally to some, while others have to work hard to acquire it.

Regardless of how much extra time players spend shooting, even the great players go into shooting slumps—periods (sometimes lasting weeks) where the ball just won't go in. For this reason, the coach must be cognizant of the mental aspects of shooting as well as the physical fundamentals. Coaches sometimes think of a player's shooting slump as a physical problem only. But a mental problem can create physical problems. For example, a player who shows symptoms of staleness may demonstrate poor mechanics. These poor mechanics often involve not using the legs enough during the shot, which is important to a consistent shot. The fatigue of a shooter can sometimes be manifested in the outside shots coming up short. The tired player will often forget the importance of the legs.

I have always felt that the mental aspects should be considered. A player with a troubled mind, whatever the cause, loses concentration when shooting the outside shot. Many things can cause that lack of focus. In college, it can be the player's studies or academic problems. It could be home or social problems. It could also be financial worries. No matter how much coaches preach to leave everything other than basketball outside of the gymnasium, players will bring problems of this magnitude with them to practice and games. A wandering mind will most definitely affect shooting.

Many different problems can affect a shooter mentally. The coach can do much to condition players' minds with positive thinking by making practice a positive experience and by keeping the importance of a game in proper perspective.

Beginning practice sessions with fun is a start. Before the commencement of the first drill, bringing the players together and sharing something humorous or motivational can get things off to a good start. Ending practice on a good note is also important. A competitive shooting drill is one good way to do this, but the coach must think of a variety of ways to end practice sessions with fun. When doing so, the coach is sending a message that basketball is just a game and that there is more to life than basketball—such as relationships. The coach is communicating that he or she enjoys being with the players. Levity and humor help players look forward to practice. Humor also loosens up the players during practice, and that alone can help a shooter's touch.

To cause shooters to relax more, coaches must do everything in their power to put a game in its proper perspective as that game relates to life. A game is only a "test" to see how well practice is going. That's all it is. Things often become out of balance when a coach tries to pump a team up by reminding the players whom they are playing the following weekend, or when a coach tries to fire the team up in the locker room before the start of the game. Homework, family, and friendships are much more important than basketball. Placing too much importance on a game can only cause more tension. Tension usually leads to tightness, and we all know what that can do for shooters. What the coach *should* get across to the players is that the reason those players came out for the team is because basketball is an enjoyable game to play. It's fun.

Develop Ambidexterity of the Hands and Feet

All of us are aware that people are born left- or right-handed. Some may know that each person has a dominant eye as well. But it is rare to find anyone who understands that the same is true for the feet. People don't realize it, but they have a favorite foot. To discover a basketball player's dominant foot, the coach should watch which foot the player leaves as the nonpivot foot when pivoting. That's the dominant foot.

The importance of hand ambidexterity to being a complete player is obvious. But ambidexterity of the feet is equally important—or perhaps more important since a player spends more time doing footwork than handling the basketball. Players who are able to pivot, drive, and fake with either foot can counter any defensive maneuver made by an opponent.

Use the Whole-Part Method of Teaching

In my early years of coaching, I attended all the clinics I could. I was like a sponge, filling my notebook with new ideas and especially new drills that I was tempted to take back with me and implement in my system. At these clinics, the other coaches and I would see a presented drill, for example, and we would all say, "Wow! I like that. How did that drill go again?" We were young and hungry to acquire information and knowledge. We were competitive and believed that through the acquisition of new drills and concepts, we were gaining an edge over the opposing coaches in our leagues who didn't attend the clinic.

When I got older, I realized that most of those drills, though good, did not suit the system I was teaching. It's kind of like shopping at a huge hardware store. They have all the tools a person could ever want and at a reasonable price. You look at a particular tool and say, "I've always wanted that," and you put it in your shopping cart. Then, after continuing to shop for another half hour, your excitement about that tool greatly diminishes. You realize, for the type of work you do around the house, the tool will be of little use. You hurry back to the aisle where you found it, put it back on the shelf, and say to yourself, "I don't need that. I won't use it very often."

Coaches have always had access to a plethora of basketball drills, not only in basketball clinics, but also in basketball magazines and books. These publications list, illustrate, and explain hundreds of drills, some of which are good and some not so good. The question is not whether a particular drill is a good one. The question a coach should be asking is, "Is this a drill that is essential to teaching the system I believe in? Is it something I'm missing that helps teach some part of my system?"

Early in my coaching career, like many young coaches, I used a lot of drills. While enlisted in the U.S. Navy, and playing on their basketball team, I witnessed a system of teaching I had never seen before. Head coach Tony Hinkle showed his team an entire play and then broke it into one-on-one, two-on-two, three-on-three, four-on-four, and finally back into the "whole" he'd started with. His method was extremely effective.

When coaching, I applied the same teaching methodology to my offense, *reverse action*. All offensive practice drills and activities were carefully and specifically designed to help teach some part of that offense. Drills were primarily used to teach fundamentals, although I tried to arrange players' movements to simulate the exact movements used in the reverse action offense. For example, to teach cutting, passing, and receiving, I had the players practice getting open at the wing position. Shooting drills contained only game shots, and those shots were executed in the positions they would occur in the offense. In other words, I didn't just use a drill because it was a good drill; I used it because it was the best drill to teach part of my system. In this way, practice became more efficient, economical, and contextual.

In the following sections, I illustrate how I used the whole-part method of teaching by first presenting the basic half-court offensive system and then showing some of the "parts" that were taught.

Reverse Action

The origin of the reverse action offense can be traced back to Sam Berry's "center to the weak side option" offense of the 1940s and 1950s. Much is being said today about triangle offense, a system that creates three-man triangles, exploits defensive weaknesses, and has tremendous balance, both for offensive rebounding and defensive transition. Sam Berry's offense was a triangle offense created well before Tex Winter (now assistant coach for the Lakers) introduced the triple-post offense. Reverse action is identical to the center option offense in principles but has a different pattern. This offense is perfectly suited to counter pressure defenses and also provides the ability to post up any forward or center (a concept promoted by this book). I will first present the pattern and then the drills that help teach it. I use the word *pattern* at the risk of implying that there is a predetermined blueprint of where players are to go. But I believe that players make plays. Therefore, any time a player believes he has an advantage, that player is free to break the pattern for the score.

The Basic Pattern

We begin with a two-guard front, one forward on each side, and the center at a low-, mid-, or high-post position (see figure 15.1). In the illustration, we have the center begin at the low post.

Player 1 passes to player 3, who gets open at the wing (using any of the four methods presented in chapter 5), specifically at the foul line extended. After passing to player 3, player 1 cuts around the outside of player 3, looking for the handoff if the defense trails. If not, player 1 continues to the baseline corner area on the strong side (see figure 15.2).

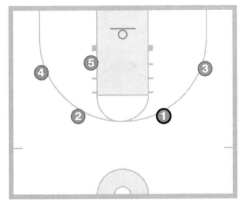

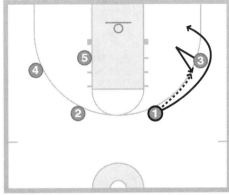

Figure 15.1 The initial set of the reverse action offense.

Figure 15.2 Player 1 passes to player 3 and cuts around, looking for the handoff pass if the defender trails.

Player 5 moves out to the weak-side wing to set a back screen for player 4. Player 5 should set the screen facing the strong side for three reasons: This position helps the player get open if his defender leaves an opening, enables the player to avoid a moving screen violation, and allows the player to get to the rebound if player 4 receives the ball and shoots after cutting off the screen. Player 4 employs one of four options when using the screen: fake over the top and cut baseline to the basket area, fake baseline and cut over the top to the opposite low post, use the same cut to come to the free throw line for the jump shot, or make either fake and pop back to the weak-side wing to receive a skip pass for the jump shot. In figure 15.3, we use the fake baseline cut and move over the top.

Player 4 uses the screen by cutting below it and then over the top, although not necessarily. Player 4 may be open for the layup. If not, the player continues to the strong-side block for the post-up (see figure 15.3).

Player 3 passes the basketball out to player 2, player 5 moves out to the wing to receive the ball, and player 3 uses player 4's back screen to cut to the strong side (see figure 15.4). Player 1 moves out to the guard position to reverse the basketball again, if necessary. Reverse action continues until

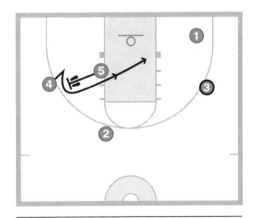

Figure 15.3 Player 5 sets a back screen for player 4, who cuts to the basket, looking for the catch and score.

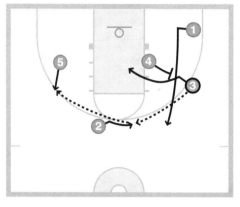 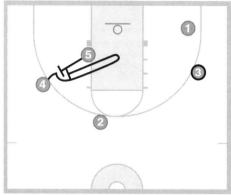

Figure 15.4 Player 3 uses player 4's screen, after player 3 passes out to player 2.

Figure 15.5 Player 4 button hooks back and sets a screen for player 5, who will cut into the key, looking for the catch and score.

a high-percentage shot is obtained. The next reversal of the basketball would give player 5 the opportunity to cut off the screen and post up. Incidentally, this is a great option because most defensive centers do not have experience being back screened on the perimeter.

Various options can be employed to take advantage of mismatches in the post. For example, after player 4 uses player 5's back screen, player 4—instead of continuing to the strong side—can button hook and set a screen for player 5, who will then cut to the other side for the post-up (see figure 15.5).

Reverse action can also be used to post up a guard. When initiating the play with the pass from player 1 to player 3, player 4 and player 2 exchange position. (Exchanges can be made any time during the play or can be set plays.) Instead of player 5 screening for player 4, the screen is set for the guard, who uses the screen to get open for the layup or to post up (see figure 15.6).

Another option, essential for all offenses, is the backdoor play. When player 5 is about to set the screen on player 4 and notices player 4's defender is playing tight, player 5 moves toward the guard and receives the pass while player 4 makes a hard cut straight to the basket. A bounce pass from player 5 to player 4 may lead to an uncontested layup.

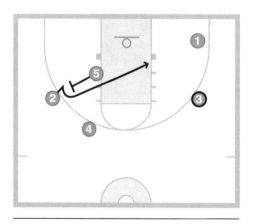

Figure 15.6 Players 4 and 2 exchange positions, and player 2 uses player 5's back screen to cut into the post.

Parts Drills

After showing the team the entire play, we divide the players into small groups that will go to different baskets to work on the parts of the play. Some of those groups may consist of just two players and one coach. Some may include three or four players.

Because the entry pass from player 1 to player 3 is so important, one of the first parts we work on is getting player 3 open to receive the ball at the free throw line extended. Here, we may use

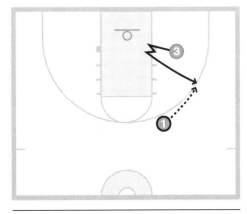

Figure 15.7 One "part" to work on is player 3 getting open to receive the pass from player 1.

one guard and one forward, or we may have the coach play the part of the passing guard and just use forwards. That will depend on if I want the guards involved in another "part" at another hoop. First without defense and then with it, we work on the four ways the forward can get open to receive the basketball (see figure 15.7). We also work on the reverse drill and some of the one-on-one options.

At another basket, I may have guards and forwards working on player 1 cutting around player 3 to go to the corner or receive the handoff pass (see figure 15.8). At a third basket, I may have the 4 and 5 players working on the reverse screen, with the coach as a passer (see figure 15.9). Because forwards are used in all three "parts," I will move players from basket to basket.

It may take several days to bring the entire team back to five-on-five. In other words, one day of practice is not enough to sufficiently work on

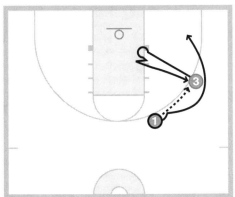

Figure 15.8 Another breakdown drill is working on player 1's cut around player 3.

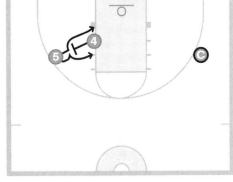

Figure 15.9 Still another part is players 4 and 5 working on the back screen.

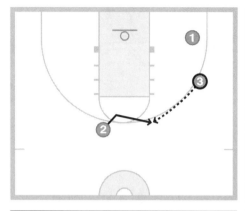 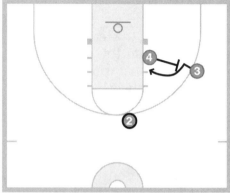

Figure 15.10 Players 2 and 3 working on the pass back out.

Figure 15.11 Players 2, 3, and 4 working on the back screen.

all the parts of a play. For example, another part that needs work is the pass back out from player 3 to player 2 (see figure 15.10), not to mention special options that we might be using in an upcoming game.

We also don't transition from simple "parts" directly into the five-on-five; we go from two-on-two to three-on-three and then to four-on-four before progressing to the whole play. An example of a three-on-three activity is working on the back screen but now including the forward as a passer (see figure 15.11).

Although the correct amount of time was spent on teaching the fundamentals through drills, the vast majority of the practice session was devoted to the whole-part method of teaching where the players could use the fundamentals to execute the play. Since basketball is a game of plays and playing, I believe players need to play basketball during practice, albeit in a controlled setting.

The use of the whole-part method is not limited to half-court offense; it can be used to teach all parts of the game, such as breaking the press, out-of-bounds plays, team defense, the fast break, and the full-court press.

Systematic Development of the Inside Game

By nature, young people are impatient. That is one reason why they are so active in attempting to create quick changes in the world. Change is good if it results in progress. All progress is change, but not all change is progress. When basketball players work on developing the inside game, progress must be made quickly or they may lose interest. The things that players are taught about how to play inside must quickly become successful in competition. Once a young person sees the benefit of the post curriculum in games, that player will become a "believer" and will be motivated for continued learning. For example, when a post move is taught and the player is successful with that move in the game, the job of the teacher is almost done.

For that reason, a systematic and progressive plan for quick and practical improvement must be instituted and followed. This plan will work equally well for the tall or the smaller player. Because the offensive moves will be tailored to the talents and strengths of the individual, results may vary. Smaller players will likely be assigned to learn moves with more finesse, and taller players will learn moves with more power. All players can learn post play, but the personal repertoire will depend on body type. For teaching offensive moves, we recommend that the systematic plan be arranged in the following order: teach the fundamentals, teach one move and a counter, implement the moves into the practice scrimmage, and implement the moves into game competition. Following is a sample program for developing low-post offensive moves. The same system can be used to teach any other part of the game.

Teach Fundamentals

Complex basketball moves are dependent on the quick and proper execution of the fundamentals. Therefore, the first step in developing low-post moves is to develop balance, footwork, maneuvering speed, and a sound base of operation and proper shooting technique for all post shots. These are presented in chapters 2, 3, 4, and 8. Daily practice of fundamentals is recommended, but this practice should only be for a few minutes. Balance, footwork, maneuvering speed, and shooting cannot be developed in a week. Small daily improvements over the course of several months will yield permanent results.

Teach One Move and a Counter

Unless students have never played basketball before, they already have a way of doing things in the post. They usually have a favorite shot or move that they use, whether it's a turnaround jump shot or a jump hook. That is OK. At this point, the coach watches to see how effective that move or shot is and determines if it can be developed into a primary move. The smaller players often use jump shots. The Sikma move (presented in chapter 9) may be the perfect primary maneuver for those players. The taller players often use turnaround moves as well. We recommend that coaches consider teaching sky hooks or jump hooks as primary moves for all players.

The primary move must be developed into a definite scoring threat. The Sikma move should be executed quickly so that instant space is created between the offensive player and the defender. For hook shots, the player must learn to create quick space vertically.

Once a primary scoring threat is developed, one countermove must be presented and practiced. Sikma 2 is the counter for Sikma 1. The baseline drop step can be a counter for the hook shot across the key. However, for the tall player, if the defender blocks the path for the hook shot across the key, a great countermove is a turn back toward the baseline for the jump shot. This counter creates instant space.

At this point, the temptation to add more counters for counters will be there. That temptation must be resisted. One main scoring move and one countermove are all a player needs to be successful. Next, with a defensive player playing any way she wants, the player practices reading the defense while initiating the main move. This type of practice is not limited to the practice session or even extracurricular sessions with the coach. Players who are passionate about improvement can get together and practice in the same way.

Implement the Moves Into the Practice Scrimmage

Practicing moves and countermoves does not eliminate the temptation to revert back to the old moves a player had. At first, when scrimmaging in practice, using the old moves will be the rule rather than the exception. In most cases, the reason for this is that the player is afraid to try the new moves for fear of failure or embarrassment. However, the coach who allows this to continue is doing the player a disservice. The transition from old habit to new will surely take a long time. And, as we mentioned, young people are impatient. Therefore, the coach must convince the player that the best way to develop the new moves is to use them exclusively in the scrimmage. When the old moves are used, the coach must immediately administer correction. On the part of the player, there will probably be a degree of reluctance. However, this is the only way that quick improvement will be realized.

Implement the Moves Into Game Competition

The temptation to regress back to the old moves and habits becomes even greater during games—when family and friends are watching. The player may not yet be completely convinced that the coach's process is beneficial in the long run. For lack of a better term, *tough love* is the best thing. Condoning the use of both the old moves and the new moves will do much more harm than good. If allowed, the player will continue to do the same, and real progress will not be achieved. There is nothing wrong with taking that player out of the game for a brief reminder of the plan. Once convinced that they will not get away with anything less than the exclusive use of the new move and countermove, most players will respond positively. This is an exciting time for the teacher, and soon will be for the student.

A systematic approach is not exclusive to basketball. Many academic curricula are designed in the same fashion. For example, the success of the "Reading A-Z" phonics program is dependent on this type of approach. On their Web site (www.readinga-z.com), it states, "Direct and explicit teaching of the major sound/symbol relationships in a specific and clearly defined sequence, known as systematic phonics, is a more effective instruction strategy than teaching phonics without a systematic order or without direct and explicit instruction."

The concept of immediate implementation into practice—for the purpose of maintaining students' interest and increasing motivation—is also not new to literacy education. In 1954, *Life Magazine* published a report on literacy among school children. This report concluded that children were not learning to read because their books were boring. Accordingly, Theodor Seuss Geisel's (Dr. Seuss) publisher made up a list of 400 words that he felt were important; he asked Dr. Seuss to cut the list to 250 words and write a book using only those words. Nine months later, Seuss, using 220 of the words given to him, completed *The Cat in the Hat*. The work was a fresh and welcome alternative to the Dick and Jane books of the day, and parents as well as teachers stormed the bookstores to buy copies. For the first time, the phonics programs of the day had material available that children were excited about, and that material bridged the gap between learning to read and reading to learn.

Conclusion

Many styles of teaching can be used in coaching; much of it depends on the personality of the coach and the methods that the coach has been previously exposed to. Some coaches, such as Bobby Knight, are extremely animated, verbally demanding, and impatient. Others, such as the Indianapolis Colts' Tony Dungy, are soft-spoken and use high expectations to generate players' self-motivation and team improvement. Both styles win championships. What matters is not the manner in which you teach; it's the principles you use to help players develop skill, conditioning, and teamwork.

I have always believed that explaining the "why" of my expectations helps players understand the big picture. I also believe it's important to be sensitive to what my players are going through off the court. Teaching ambidexterity, for me, is nonnegotiable. The whole-part method of teaching has been a key to my success and the success of many other coaches. For teaching post moves, the systematic way of teaching is the most effective way to make new material practical.

It has been said, "Teach a player to shoot well and he's all ears from that point on." I believe that. At the Big Man Camp and Tall Women's Camp, we have seen miracles happen in one week because what we teach players works in competition immediately. The same can happen for the high school and college coach.

INDEX

ABOUT THE AUTHORS

Pete Newell has a collegiate coaching record of 234-123, including back-to-back appearances in the NCAA championship game (1959 and 1960) with the University of California at Berkeley. He won one NCAA title, an NIT title, and a gold medal with the 1960 U.S. team. Newell's Cal teams won four consecutive Pacific-8 titles (1957-1960), and Newell was National Coach of the Year in 1960. Considered America's "basketball guru" for his vast knowledge and teaching skills, Newell was enshrined in the Naismith Basketball Hall of Fame in 1979. He has run his Big Man Camp since 1976 and his Tall Women's Camp since 2001, developing the skills of serious high school, collegiate, and professional players.

Swen Nater is a former NBA and ABA center who led both leagues in rebounding and who is often consulted as a big man's coach for developing high school and college players. Nater, who developed his post skills under the tutelage of John Wooden at UCLA, runs his own Big Man Camp in Seattle, where he has helped to develop many players who have gone on to play in the NBA. He also works as an instructor at Pete Newell's Big Man Camp and has authored three basketball instructional books, including one on rebounding.

Photo by Todd Cheney/UCLA Photography